Shakespeare in the Present

Shakespeare in the Present: Political Lessons under Biden is the first case study in applying the lessons of Shakespeare's plays to post-Trump America. It looks at American politics through the lens of Shakespeare, not simply equating figures in the contemporary world to Shakespearean characters, but showing how the broader conditions of Shakespeare's imagined worlds reflect and inform our own. Clearly written, in a direct and engaging style, it shows that reading Shakespeare with our contemporary Washington in mind can enrich our understanding of both his works and our world. Shakespeare wrote for his own time, but we always read him in our present. As such, the way we read him now is always affected by our own understanding of our own political world. This book provides quick critical analyses of Shakespeare's plays and contemporary American politics while serving as an introduction for undergraduates and general readers to this kind of topical, presentist criticism of Shakespeare.

Philip Goldfarb Styrt is an Assistant Professor of English at St. Ambrose University in Davenport, IA. He received his Ph.D. in English from the University of Chicago in 2015, and his first book, *Shakespeare's Political Imagination: The Historicism of Setting* was published in 2021.

Routledge Focus on Literature

Masculinities in Post-Millennial Popular Romance
Eirini Arvanitaki

A Glimpse at the Travelogues of Baghdad
Iman Al-Attar

Shakespeare in the Present
Political Lessons under Biden
Philip Goldfarb Styrt

Speech Acts in Blake's Milton
Brian Russell Graham

Literature, Education, and Society
Bridging the Gap
Charles F. Altieri

Shakespeare and the Theater of Pity
Shawn Smith

Trauma, Memory and Silence of the Irish Woman in Contemporary Literature
Wounds of the Body and the Soul
Edited by Madalina Armie and Verónica Membrive

For more information about this series, please visit: www.routledge.com/Routledge-Focus-on-Literature/book-series/RFLT

Shakespeare in the Present
Political Lessons under Biden

Philip Goldfarb Styrt

Routledge
Taylor & Francis Group

NEW YORK AND LONDON

First published 2023
by Routledge
605 Third Avenue, New York, NY 10158

and by Routledge
4 Park Square, Milton Park, Abingdon, Oxon, OX14 4RN

Routledge is an imprint of the Taylor & Francis Group, an informa business

ISBN: 978-1-032-36324-0 (hbk)
ISBN: 978-1-032-36328-8 (pbk)
ISBN: 978-1-003-33139-1 (ebk)

DOI: 10.4324/9781003331391

Typeset in Times New Roman
by MPS Limited, Dehradun

Contents

Acknowledgments

Thanks to my wife, Katie Styrt, for listening when I babbled about this, and my daughter Helen, for also being there. Thanks also to the organizers of the 2021 Enemies in the Early Modern World conference at the University of Edinburgh, where much of the "lost France" material began, and to Jackie Cameron, Eric Johnson, and the rest of the Shakespeare and France seminar at the 2022 SAA conference, where it took on its presentist tinge.

Introduction: Shakespeare and Biden

Joe Biden is the oldest-ever president of the United States. But despite his age, neither he nor even the United States itself was anywhere near existing when William Shakespeare wrote his plays over four hundred years ago. So why on earth should we look at Shakespeare's plays to help understand the political world of Biden's presidency?

One answer is that we always have. Maybe not about Biden's presidency, but ever since Shakespeare's own time people have been reading, performing, and generally thinking about the contemporary lessons of his plays.[1] What "contemporary" might mean has shifted over that time, of course. When Elizabeth I supposedly said "I am Richard II, know ye not that?" a statement that many critics have connected to a performance of Shakespeare's *Richard II*, she would have been talking about a recent play potentially written or at least performed about her.[2] When I argue, as I do here, that the same play has implications for Biden's presidency as well, I am obviously not suggesting that *Richard II* was written about Biden. Instead, I am arguing, as people have for centuries, that there is something about the way Shakespeare imagines his worlds that makes his plays still speak to us even across the ever-widening gap of years, and that how we read Shakespeare is always connected to what is going on in our own world. So despite the fact that the political world of twenty-first century America is unlike that of sixteenth-century England—or the fourteenth-century England where *Richard II* is set—something about the people Shakespeare sketches and the way they react to their own situations is still deeply human, and deeply relevant to us.

In other words, Shakespeare's insights into human character, politics, and the absurdities that these two create when combined are still applicable today, even though the world has shifted. This doesn't mean that we can just slap a label on Shakespeare's Richard II that says "Joe Biden" any more than we could do so with "Elizabeth I" (she

DOI: 10.4324/9781003331391-1

was not *literally* Richard II, after all). But it does mean that once we understand what is going on in *Richard II*—and now—we can see how Richard's reaction to *his* situation can inform Biden's to his own, or ours to Biden's actions.

We always read Shakespeare in the present. We cannot read it any other time. And it matters for us in the present not just because people have been reading it for a long time, or because Shakespeare is famous, but because it still manages to connect to us and our time.

This, then, is my answer to the question I posed above. We look for wisdom in the present from Shakespeare not because he was a prophet for our times, but because he paid so much attention to the way people thought and acted in their own times that his plays still speak to us now. It is precisely because Shakespeare did not try to write universal plays that his plays might be widely applicable. His colleague Ben Jonson wrote that Shakespeare was "not of an age, but for all time", but that is a false choice.[3] Shakespeare is always both: the plays he wrote are deeply and specifically invested in the worlds they represent, and it is *because* of that they are able to speak to other times and places, from his to ours.

This is particularly true with respect to politics. We often think of politics as ephemeral: here today, and gone tomorrow. A vote is passed, and it is done; an election happens and (hopefully) we know the result and move forward; a speech is made and recorded, and only needs to be referenced when writing the history books decades later. But while a given political moment is indeed fleeting, the situations of politics repeat. This does not necessarily happen in predictable ways, such as Karl Marx's "the first time as tragedy, the second as farce," but over and over we see similar questions being asked of those in the historical spotlight.[4] And while the details of each moment are significant, and often significantly different, we can still see in Shakespeare a guide to what might work—or what will not work at all.

In the chapters that follow, I will take a look at several political crises and situations of the present political moment, from the Big Lie of Biden's predecessor, Donald Trump, to the decision to withdraw US troops from Afghanistan, and show how Shakespeare's plays cast light on the decisions Biden made or might make and their consequences. In each case, I suggest that one or two plays are particularly relevant to contemporary circumstances, though I do not hesitate to draw more broadly where Shakespeare wrote repeatedly on similar themes. As such, each chapter takes a dive into the world of at least one Shakespeare play while also explaining how the decisions the characters make in that world are applicable to the present.

The first chapter situates Biden's presidency within the partisan political polarization of the modern electorate. The kind of deep-seated factional division we see today between Republicans and Democrats in America is a favorite theme of Shakespeare's, particularly in his Roman tragedies and his English histories. Drawing on these plays, this chapter argues that for Shakespeare the worst way to approach this kind of political division is to try to pretend it does not exist. Those like Brutus and Henry VI who attempt to bridge the divide between factions without understanding the depth of their division are doomed to fail; only those, like Antony and Edward IV, who respond with clear-eyed awareness of the divided state can succeed. This suggests that the proper attitude towards contemporary politics is not optimism about bipartisanship but a stark assessment of who is on which side—and of the very real dangers of political violence associated with that partisanship.

The next chapter develops this theme by looking more deeply at the abortive attempt to keep Trump in office that led to the January 6, 2021 insurrection. This is where *Richard II* comes in: I argue that in that play Shakespeare shows the danger of tolerating pretextual legal claims that disguise a larger attempt to overthrow the state. I then develop this further to show, through *Coriolanus* and *Much Ado About Nothing*, that Shakespeare cautions against the dangers of disputed elections, specifically, and of not punishing those who attempt to overthrow the state when they fail. Don John's willingness to betray Don Pedro again in *Much Ado* even after being forgiven suggests that Biden ought not to ignore the potential for further danger from the same people who attempted to undo his election.

From the discord between Republicans and Democrats I then turn to other domestic political concerns in the next three chapters. First, I suggest that our approach to the expectations facing Biden after his election might be informed by Prince Hal's transformation into Henry V. This suggests that the assumptions others will make about how Biden acts will always be shaped by who he was before, and both we and he must take that into account. In this regard, I also connect Biden's public negotiations over the Build Back Better Act to the difficulties King Lear experiences after his failed love test at the start of that play. In the following chapter, I explore Shakespeare's attitude towards the weaknesses of alliances that fail to hold all their members together, arguing that Joe Manchin and Kyrsten Sinema have much in common with Warwick, Clarence, and Buckingham in the War of the Roses cycle. Political alliances are broken, I suggest, less by broad disagreements than by specific flashpoints—and breaking them is dangerous for all parties. I then consider the current disputes about the legitimacy of the Supreme Court, arguing that Shakespeare's *Henry VIII, Merchant of Venice,* and *Measure for Measure* suggest that the answer to a stacked court is not to cling to historical norms but to engage in some kind of retaliatory action, such as court-packing.

Finally, I turn towards Biden's foreign policy, and how Shakespeare's plays can inform our thinking about how pundits have reacted to it. I suggest that the accusations that Biden "lost" Afghanistan (and now that he might "lose" Ukraine) are closely related to those about how England "lost" France, in that one cannot lose what was never fully yours—and that claims about having done so are a part of domestic politics, not foreign policy. This in turn suggests that we should be extremely wary of such claims in the present, particularly if they threaten to drag us into further ineffectual or damaging wars—as they did for Shakespeare's English in France.

Throughout this book, I suggest that the way we should interpret these parallels is complex, but the lessons they ultimately offer are simple. We should read the plays carefully on their own terms, and only then move on to think about how they relate to our own time. But when we do so, we see that Shakespeare has laid out a clear path for the sorts of situations we see in the current moment. Be aware of who is on your side and why; make actions have consequences; be clear about what you wish to achieve. As we shall see, these are the kinds of lessons Shakespeare holds for Biden, and for us, as long as we are clear about the circumstances facing us.

Notes

1 See, for extended American examples, Kim C. Sturgess, *Shakespeare and the American Nation* (Cambridge: Cambridge University Press, 2004); James Schapiro, *Shakespeare in a Divided America* (New York: Penguin Press, 2020).

2 Recent scholars have complicated the connection between Shakespeare's *Richard II* and this comment, but the idea that Shakespeare's plays were subject to topical application in their own time is relatively uncontroversial. For a good discussion of this quote's provenance and meaning, see Jason Scott-Warren, "Was Elizabeth I Richard II? The Authenticity of Lambarde's 'Conversation'," *The Review of English Studies* New Series 64, no. 264 (2013): 208–230.

3 Ben Jonson, "To the memory of my beloved, The Author Mr. William Shakespeare And what he hath left us," in *Mr. VVilliam Shakespeare's comedies, histories, & tragedies Published according to the true original copies* (London: Isaac Iaggard and Ed. Blount, 1623), n.p.

4 Karl Marx, *The Eighteenth Brumaire of Louis Bonaparte, With Explanatory Notes* (New York: International Publishers, 1963), 15.

References

Jonson, Ben. "To the memory of my beloved, The Author Mr. William Shakespeare And what he hath left us." In *Mr. VVilliam Shakespeare's Comedies, Histories, & Tragedies Published According to the True Original Copies*, n.p. London: Isaac Iaggard and Ed. Blount, 1623.

Marx, Karl. *The Eighteenth Brumaire of Louis Bonaparte, With Explanatory Notes*. New York: International Publishers, 1963.

Schapiro, James. *Shakespeare in a Divided America*. New York: Penguin Press, 2020.

Scott-Warren, Jason. "Was Elizabeth I Richard II? The Authenticity of Lambarde's 'Conversation'," *The Review of English Studies* New Series 64, no. 264 (2013): 208–230.

Sturgess, Kim C. *Shakespeare and the American Nation*. Cambridge: Cambridge University Press, 2004.

1 Partisan Polarization

A common—and correct—analysis of politics today is that we are living in a time of partisan polarization: a time when politics is a struggle between two parties, those parties disagree about major public issues, and membership in those groups is becoming regimented. This is a situation that feels new to us, but that Shakespeare wrote about repeatedly. Precisely because this was a common theme in Shakespeare, I suggest that looking at what he has to say about living in and governing for such a society can help us find productive ways to think about public life in our own America.

In particular, I suggest we can draw three lessons from Shakespeare about politics in a time of partisan polarization. The first, and most critical, is the danger of naïveté. It is vital to not only understand the political realities of this brave new world of polarization but to acknowledge them practically. The second point is related: the importance of adaptability. Treating the present like the past will only end in tragedy. And finally, I argue that Shakespeare's plays show that we cannot understate the dangers of polarized politics. While we must always remember that the worlds Shakespeare draws are not actually our own—even if they can help us think about our own—it is worth noting that the two most polarized countries he put on stage both ended up resolving the polarization not by coming to a comfortable accommodation but by war followed by the institution of an entirely new regime.

I do not write this to suggest that Shakespeare teaches us that there will be a second American Civil War if we continue down the current path. I do not think such a simple equation of situation with situation is valid. Rather, I want to argue that observing what Shakespeare does with his divided Romes and Englands better equips us to think about our own divided America—wherever it may be headed.

DOI: 10.4324/9781003331391-2

Polarization in late republican Rome

Late republican Rome, just before it became an empire, was an extremely divided state. For decades, opposing factions fought against each other for control. The leaders of these factions changed, but the basic division did not. Whether it was Sulla fighting Marius, Julius Caesar fighting Pompey, or Marc Antony fighting Octavius (later the emperor Augustus), the period was one of constant partisan division, frequently breaking into outright warfare.

Shakespeare set two of his Roman plays in this period—*Julius Caesar* and *Antony and Cleopatra*—and he and his contemporaries were extremely sensitive to the importance of the divisions in the state during this period. While we would use the term "party" for these organized bands of political allies, the dominant term in the Elizabethan period was "faction." Both *Julius Caesar* and *Antony and Cleopatra* are well-aware of the factions in their politics. Antony perhaps explains it best in the play bearing his name: "Equality of two domestic powers/Breed scrupulous faction" (1.3.47–8).[1] Likewise, Brutus and his friends who assassinate Caesar in *Julius Caesar* self-identify as a "faction" (2.1.77). These factions are the functional reality of the late Roman republic, entrenched parties with directly opposing interests: that is, Shakespeare's Rome is polarized by party just as America is today.

And yet, the Roman republic was not intended to work this way. Just as George Washington warned early Americans about the dangers of a two-party system, the early Roman republic was not factionally divided—or at least not in the strongly polarized sense that it is in *Julius Caesar* and *Antony and Cleopatra*. Cassius and Brutus in particular remind us repeatedly throughout their play of this earlier politics, most notably through the references to Brutus's ancestor Junius Brutus, who led the revolt that overthrew the king who ruled before the republic (1.2.160–2, 2.1.53–5). For Shakespearean Rome, just as for modern America, the realities of partisan politics clash with the ideal of high-minded statesmen doing their best for the nation and overthrowing tyranny for the good of all.

However, a dominant message of these Roman plays is that those who try to re-enact this ideal past in the present are doomed to failure. We can see this in *Julius Caesar* through the contrast between Brutus's political instincts and Cassius's. These two are on the same side, but their political understandings are diametrically opposed. For Brutus, the politics of the early republic are always within reach, if Rome will but stretch out its hand and grasp them. This is what Antony eulogizes over Brutus's corpse, the belief that somehow Rome is truly united underneath all the factional division, and that if he can just get rid of Caesar Brutus can somehow call back the less polarized, less partisan past (5.5.70–1). He continually imagines Rome this way, and it informs his political failures, from thinking Antony can do nothing without Caesar (and so forbidding Cassius from killing them together) to allowing Antony to speak at Caesar's funeral (which leads directly to a violent mob hunting down Brutus's allies and tearing them to pieces) (2.1.161–2, 3.1.232–5).

Cassius is not so foolish. He wants to kill Antony precisely because he recognizes that partisan polarization between the Roman factions means Antony can lead the Caesarean faction after its leader's death. He tries to dissuade Brutus from allowing Antony to speak to the people after the assassination because he sees the danger in allowing the other faction to spin the situation. Notably, Cassius is shown to be the more cunning politician of the two of them even before they disagree about these strategies, as he tricks Brutus into believing Rome is more united against Caesar than it is in order to convince him to formally throw in his lot with the anti-Caesarean faction. Similarly, he stage-manages Brutus hearing about an off-stage scene where Caesar was offered (and refused) a crown, making sure that it is only their ally Caska and not any of the other characters who talk about the event, which is deliberately misinterpreted (1.2.180–2).

But because of the zero-sum nature of partisan polarization, Cassius's underhanded yet effective tactics end up replaced by Brutus's more candid, less effective ones. Brutus misunderstands how Roman politics works. But Brutus is also the public face of the faction. As such, his words have extra weight, and it is he who decides to overrule Cassius's plans about Antony. The two-faction system, and Brutus's place in it, mean that no matter how well Cassius understands Roman politics, he cannot do anything until he convinces Brutus to do it too.[2]

Of course, Caesar's party has the same problem. Like Brutus, Caesar does not quite grasp how polarized Roman politics is—though for opposite reasons. He thinks this is because everyone loves him, as opposed to because everyone hates him, but he is equally wrong. Brutus ignores Cassius's advice about Antony, and Caesar too ignores everyone whose better instincts tell him to avoid the Capitol and his future death, from the eerie sayings of the soothsayer to the wishes of his wife Calpurnia and the practical advice Artemidorus tries to pass him at the last minute (1.2.25–6, 2.2.104–5, 3.1.6–9). Before his death, the Caesarean party can no more control Caesar than the conspirators can control Brutus, and each party is the weaker for it.

The difference is that once Caesar is assassinated, Marc Antony takes over the Caesarean party, and Antony's political instincts are much cannier than Brutus's (at least in this play). Antony is brutally aware of the polarized nature of Roman politics and weaponizes that knowledge, first inspiring a mob to roam the streets looking for conspirators and then literally publishing a list of those to be killed for their political leanings (3.2.246–52, 3.3.5–38, 4.1.1–9). He wages a successful war to destroy the conspirators, whose efforts to defend themselves are complicated once again by an inability to act together. At the end of the play, the anti-Caesarean party is utterly crushed because it has run up against a political operative who actually understands and appreciates the power of partisanship in this world.

Shakespeare revisited that world a decade later in *Antony and Cleopatra*, with a similar theme in mind—only this time it is Antony who now misunderstands just how divided Rome is against itself. If we look carefully, we can see this change developing at the very end of *Julius Caesar*, as Antony and Octavius (later Augustus Caesar) divide up the followers of the dead Brutus and Cassius (5.5.60). Antony seems to take this as an end to the polarization of Rome—but both history and the physical sight of the actors forming into two groups on stage make it clear that the partisanship has merely shifted from the conspirators against Caesareans to Antony against Octavius.

This conspicuous divide between parties is picked back up in *Antony and Cleopatra*, which begins only a little while after *Julius Caesar* ended. There we see Antony and Octavius literally dividing the Roman world between them. While for a little while they are capable of uniting to fend off other threats, everyone in the society can see the collision between the two sides coming (as an aside, the brief mention, in both plays, of Lepidus, the third historical triumvir along with Antony and Octavius, and his equally quick dismissal from the plot, serve to highlight the uselessness of third parties in this divide). Antony and Octavius have staked out not only literal territory but also the metaphorical divisions between their parties: this time Antony takes the part of traditional "nobility" assigned to Brutus in *Julius Caesar*, while it is now Octavius who is the cunning operator.

The language used to describe Antony in the later play sounds like that he used for Brutus, so it should not be a surprise that he shows a similar failure to understand the shifting times. In a sense, however, his failures are more like Caesar's. Like Caesar, Antony likes to imagine himself above the partisan bickering of his time, and like him he is wrong. However, in Antony's case this takes the form not of trying to bring the factions together in a way that gets him killed, like Caesar does, but of trying to deny his own role in the factional world in a way that makes him ridiculous and brings about his own downfall.

The ghost of Pompey the Great haunts both these plays, and both plays refer back to him repeatedly.[3] What Pompey represents is that very partisan polarization, that factional history, that the characters so frequently want to forget. Pompey and Caesar briefly divided the Roman world between them (along with Crassus, historically associated with the same faction as Pompey) before waging war on each other. The repeated references to Pompey, most of all his son Sextus's defeat in *Antony and Cleopatra*, ask us to remember that this is an ongoing and continual process of factional warfare and displacement: that there is no way out of the factional wars but by death.

Antony at his best remembers this. He is the one who first brings up faction in the play, and connects this specifically to the rise of Sextus Pompey. Indeed, there is a period in the play—say between 1.4 and 3.2—when it almost seems as if Sextus Pompey's presence has brought the play back to a time when the factions in question were Pompey and Caesar and not Octavius Caesar and Antony. Caesar and Antony in this time speak of each other as allies, as we saw them do in *Julius Caesar*. And they do indeed come together to deal with Sextus Pompey's threat to their joint government. But even as they do so, Enobarbus correctly notes what is happening: they will deal with Pompey and then turn on each other (2.2.110–2). The interlude with Pompey is not a new start for Caesar and Antony, but a last gasp of their old connection. Even though Antony marries Caesar's sister Octavia as an attempt to reinvigorate their alliance, he immediately leaves her with the news that despite their marriage he is planning to go to war with her brother (3.3.25–8).

And yet even as he wages war on Caesar, Antony seems to be caught flatfooted by the very concept that should have been most obvious to him: that Caesar is not just Caesar, but part of a faction. He relies primarily upon his own strength and power, supplemented by Cleopatra's, and disregards the fact that it is not merely a battle of individuals but of factions. Enobarbus tries his best to remind him that Caesar's people, and Antony's people, matter to this fight but he shrugs him off (3.7.30–54). He seems surprised to learn that Caesar's forces can conquer when Caesar himself is absent (3.7.56–7). But he should know that Caesar has lieutenants, as he himself does, to do his bidding.

This is, I think, what the play frequently refers to as Antony being no longer being himself, and forgetting himself. It is not that Antony has actually changed; it is that he has forgotten how he fits into the larger world. After he loses a major battle to Caesar, he literally dismisses his friends (a term laden with political as well as personal significance in this play as in *Julius Caesar*⁴) and tells them he will not make use of them any further. His apparent reason for this is his desire to live either in Egypt with Cleopatra or, failing that, as a "private man in Athens" (3.12.15). But these desires ignore who Antony really is: not just a man, who can do as other men might and retire when he wishes, but the leader of a faction. He may have pushed away his allies, but they cannot (and Caesar will not) pretend Antony is not their leader. After Caesar denies his request to live apart from the political world, Antony once again dares his rival to a single combat (3.13.25–29). But this is just a much a misunderstanding of his situation as the desire to leave; Caesar has no need to face him one on one because their factions are already locked in continual combat. Antony berates Caesar's envoy for Caesar's "harping on what I am,/Not what he knew I was" (3.13.144–5). Yet the problem here is Antony's own unwillingness to admit what he is.

In this sense, Antony's factional errors are like Brutus's in *Julius Caesar*: failures of imagination. Brutus imagines Caesar as a unique figure standing apart from the factional world; Antony thinks the same of himself. And they fail precisely because they cannot properly approach the problems they face with this incomplete understanding of the political world around them. The factional worlds of *Julius Caesar* and *Antony and Cleopatra* are too politically polarized for Brutus or the later Antony—or perhaps it is more accurate to say that neither of them can see the partisanship properly for what it is.

Caesar and Antony beyond Trump

The application of these Roman plays to contemporary American politics is more frequent than an uninformed observer might imagine. Recently, and famously, a 2017 production of *Julius Caesar* by the Public Theater in New York (as Shakespeare in the Park) became a flashpoint for partisan disagreement about the presidency of Donald Trump—and for later thinkpieces about Shakespeare and America—by casting a Caesar who looked and acted like the then-president.⁵ The Public's portrayal does have lessons for us about how Trump might be like Caesar. But in the context of the readings of Roman party politics I've sketched above, Trump looks less like Caesar than he does Cassius or the later Antony: less the triumphant ruler who looks down on party politics than the canny navigator of those same political currents who nevertheless falls afoul of the very dynamics he himself had earlier whipped up.

Caesar looks to a post-partisan age. This is his great flaw in the play that bears his name; he fails to see that while he is on top now, his victory is not eternal. In his brief half-play of life we see him repeatedly extend the olive branch of peace and post-partisan reconciliation to those who will, in the end, knife him down.

Can we imagine Trump ever doing the same? Perhaps we could imagine Caesar, like Trump, telling the assembled multitude that "I alone can fix it,"[6] but I would suggest that (unlike Trump) Caesar imagined himself achieving his goals not over the protestations of his opponents but with them alongside him. Caesar thought himself unique, as Trump does, but in a very different way.

I argue that instead we see in Trump the same instincts that briefly raise Cassius to near the heights Trump actually reached. The man who was fact-checked daily by multiple publications might have reason to envy Cassius's easy ability to fool Brutus by simply throwing into his window some forged letters (1.2.315–22)—or perhaps Cassius would have reason to envy Trump's ability to use similar techniques not to introduce another leader to his faction but to cement his own control.

Obviously there are flaws with both comparisons, but that points back, I think, to the larger point about how we should read Shakespeare's plays as commenting on our own time (as they did on his own). It is not as simple as taking a given character—Caesar, Cassius—and equating them with a contemporary politician. This is attractive because it is simple. But precisely because it is simple, it is deceptive, and the comparison always has its limits. At its worst, this becomes what Jeffrey Wilson, following Scott Newstok and Harry Berger, has called "citational opportunism": the desire to grab at Shakespeare for any perceived equivalence, without regard to larger context.[7] Not all parallels are citational opportunism, of course, but the temptation towards simplification can easily err in that direction. We can see the difficulty inherent in these kinds of comparisons, for instance, in Yu Jin Ko's inability to decide whether Trump or Steve Bannon is more Falstaff or more Hal (from the *Henry IV* plays).[8] Neither is truly either; the specifics of the parallel are less important than the more general circumstances indicated by the comparison.

Rather than looking for this kind of direct correspondence between Shakespearean characters and modern equivalents, it is better to look at the weight of the overall circumstances he presents and the lessons they can give us relative to the contemporary situation that we face. As I have argued elsewhere, this is how Shakespeare himself treated the burning issue of the succession crisis under Elizabeth I in *King John*: by rejecting any direct comparison between John and Elizabeth and instead focusing on the way that the very question of the disputed succession is itself toxic.[9]

How might we apply this to Shakespeare's Rome and our own America? First, I suggest it ought to draw our attention away from the characters and towards their political reality. Like our America, Rome was intensely divided; like our America, there were still those who tried their best to pretend that it was not—whether cynically, as we might suspect Caesar does by trying to move past partisan divides in service of his own goals, or sincerely, as Antony suggests to us that Brutus does. But all the characters who think this way, for whatever reason they think it, end badly. This kind of naïve belief is marked specifically as anachronistic, either a yearning for the lost glory days of Junius Brutus who slew a tyrant, or a premature hope for an imperial settlement that reunites the partisan sides under a single ruler. By not recognizing their own present, they fail, bringing doom to themselves and destroying any hope of achieving their larger goals.

At the same time, these characters are offered many opportunities to adapt. Caesar alone is given multiple chances to avoid going to the Capitol for his assassination, up to and including a letter that unveils the conspiracy itself—which Caesar never reads. Brutus repeatedly turns down Cassius's advice, always to his detriment. In the later play, Antony too has frequent opportunities to turn aside from the path to failure. Yet his solutions to his problems never fully grapple with his role as a leader of a faction, not an individual, so he, like Brutus, continually moves in the wrong direction. So in each case, we see the characters continue on their self-destructive paths despite the chance to do otherwise.

In terms of contemporary politics, then, I suggest the lessons of Shakespeare's Roman plays focus more on the process of how Biden and his allies should approach the polarized politics of the day and less on the details of who might be cosplaying Julius Caesar. On the campaign trail, candidate and even president-elect Biden showed a tendency to argue that Republicans would return to their old ways when he became president: that they would stop obstructing and there would be bipartisan compromise again.[10] The overall effect was a promise of a return to normal politics, though, given the history of the Tea Party and Obama, it might be fair to ask how normal those politics truly were. Reading Shakespeare's Roman plays carefully would suggest that this approach would be a mistake. It is true that there was more bipartisanship in Biden's earlier days in the Senate; it is also true that there was less factionalism in the time of Brutus's distant ancestors. But neither of them can return to those days through self-will alone, and the opposing faction is not likely to join them.

To be fair, as president Biden has shown more willingness to move forward without the Republican party, or at least without requiring Republicans on board; the use of Senate budget reconciliation and party-line votes in the House of Representatives have been a major focus of Biden's early presidency, and the elimination of the Senate filibuster has even been suggested. This speaks to the flip side of Shakespeare's Roman lessons: the value of learning from past experience.

If we credit Biden's statements when he was not yet president, or early on in his presidency, as reflecting the naïveté that Shakespeare warns against, his later actions seem to guard against the second accusation of an unwillingness to adapt to new situations, at least to some degree. Unlike Caesar, Brutus, and the later Antony, Biden has not ignored the warning signs that his initial political instincts might be wrong. Rather, he has accepted the limitations of the partisan polarization that he has encountered and moved his expectations. The Build Back Better Act was never going to receive the ten Republican votes necessary to break a filibuster in the Senate, but it was never asked to: the entirety of the negotiations surrounding the bill's framework centered on cementing the fifty Democratic votes (along with Vice-President Harris) needed to pass through reconciliation. The Bipartisan Infrastructure Framework did receive Republican votes, but—so far at least—Biden has not allowed that single bipartisan accomplishment to color his willingness to go about trying to achieve other goals in spite of direct Republican opposition.

At the same time, the example of Brutus and Antony speaking over Caesar's corpse—one of the most memorable moments in *Julius Caesar*—as well as the fate of Antony after his victory over Brutus' faction remind us that even if all seems well, nothing is guaranteed to remain so. The results of the 2021 off-year elections might drive this home: Virginia backed Biden comfortably but elected a Republican governor and House of Delegates only a year later. So just as it is crucial not to naïvely pretend that there is no partisan polarization, we can see that it is also vital not to assume that the polarization that does exist will continue to benefit one side. Just because the people are divided into factions does not mean that one faction will always dominate, no matter what each side has imagined over the years.[11] Brutus loses the people; Antony loses Rome. There is always the potential for the partisan playing field to shift.

These lessons are larger than this one moment in time. Shakespeare's plays speak to us not with the intense specificity of a thinkpiece but with the accumulated wisdom of experience: the experience of (fully imagined) other people in another time. Shakespeare's Rome is relevant to Biden's America not because this narrow moment in our political history closely mirrors the one that Shakespeare wrote of but because the parts of that world that echo in ours are so carefully measured on their own terms. No one (I hope) is planning to cut down Joe Biden, or Donald Trump, on the steps of the Capitol, and we should not expect to see Jill Biden or Melania Trump gather an asp to their bosom. The parallels are not so exact, nor so demanding. If, as Ohio Republican senatorial candidate J. D. Vance alleges, "we are in a late republican period," we should not look for a Caesar to save or doom us.[12] Rather, we should see how Shakespeare's divided Rome comes to grief because of an inability to grapple with the political realities of its own present, and so respond to the same danger here at home, even though the particular details of our political structure, worldview, and history are different.

Partisanship closer to home

Rome was not the only place where Shakespeare worked out the implications of partisan polarization. English history had its own examples, which Shakespeare repeatedly put on stage, most notably in the three *Henry VI* plays and *Richard III*. In these plays we see similar patterns play out against a very different backdrop. Instead of the falling republic and rising empire of Rome, with their emphasis on pre-existing partisanship, we see newly emerging partisan divides split feudal England down the middle.

There are no fixed partisan divides at the beginning of *1 Henry VI*. That is not to say that everything in England is all sunshine and rainbows. In fact, things have already begun to fall apart after the death of Henry V, as we will examine later when we take a look at the "lost France" trope in those plays and its relationship to Biden-era foreign policy. But those problems are not yet linked to a partisan division; instead all is personal and individual, as Shakespeare's Brutus imagines things having been like in the early republic. Cardinal Bedford hates Duke Humphrey of Gloucester, as do several of the other lords, if less intently; there are repeated squabbles over who was responsible for which failure in the wars in France; no one much cares for the extremely young king, except possibly the doomed Humphrey. None of these hatreds and disagreements are institutionalized, however. Each of them is the result of individual interpersonal conflict.

This shifts, however, in the course of the play, and the shift will have profound impacts through the *Henry VI* plays and into *Richard III* (as well as in actual English history, of course).[13] In 2.4 York and Somerset get into an argument about law—one that seems just as significant and just as inconsequential as all the other disagreements among the nobles in the play—and force those listening to them to pick sides: literally, in that they are asked to pick between a white rose (York) or red (Somerset) to indicate their preference.

This might seem like a minor detail to us, but to Shakespeare's audience this would have been instantly recognizable as historically significant: the white rose and the red, after all, give their name to the Wars of the Roses, the decades-long struggle between the houses of York and Lancaster for the throne that ended only with the rise of the Tudor dynasty under which Shakespeare wrote. As Stephen Greenblatt has noted, this is the point when the play's interpersonal disagreements rapidly shift into partisan polarization, starting with the king himself, who plucks a red rose (almost at random, it seems, in the play, though justified in a historical context) and aligns himself against York.[14]

Most of *1 Henry VI* is made up of the more interpersonal, highly individual conflict that centers on Duke Humphrey. But as Shakespeare moved further into the history of the period, the dynamics of the infighting changed. The two houses of Lancaster and York became, in modern terms, political parties.

In *2 Henry VI* and *3 Henry VI*, we can see the opposing political machinations of these two parties developing through at first a kind of proxy warfare and then outright violence between the two sides. As the civil war progresses, it becomes increasingly clear that this is not about a personal conflict between the leaders but an armed factional divide between their larger parties. Henry VI's attempts to end the war are a good gauge of this: he is perpetually trying to assuage the concerns of Richard of York personally, going so far as to name York his heir, but neither faction is willing to accept the end of conflict so easily, even if York himself were to be appeased.

Along the way, we see how the state of England itself is being ripped in two by the increasingly broad factional violence. In 2.5 of *3 Henry VI*, Henry VI himself watches sons kill fathers and families ripped apart. In *2 Henry VI*, York pays Jack Cade, a working-class conman with a fictionalized noble past, to rile up the lower classes against the upper, a revolt that turns from a carefully stage-managed crisis for York to exploit into a genuine danger (and then, in turn, a farce). The Earl of Warwick and the Duke of Clarence (the latter one of York's sons) move between the sides, as we will discuss at more length later, but it is clear that when they do they are seen as traitors to those they left behind—there is no space for personal conviction or private injury in the politics of these plays. Rather, every action is always public, always part of the larger divisions that have suddenly sprouted up within Shakespeare's medieval England.

By the time of *Richard III* the Yorkist party is ascendant. But the scars of this political division have not healed, and the paranoid world Richard first exploits and then succumbs to is a result of this. Everyone is constantly reminding each other of what each did when they fought Henry VI, and of course there remain factions within the court just as we saw factionalism resurrect between Octavius and Antony. Richard and his allies hate Queen Elizabeth and hers, and the division is marked as being related to their prior factional associations—even though both are clearly Yorkists at this point.

The factional division is finally resolved by the marriage at the end of *Richard III* between the future Henry VII and Elizabeth of York, and it returns us to the imagery of the white rose and the red, now united in the Tudor rose. This resolution also reminds us that—just as with the Roman plays—this period of factional division was marked for Shakespeare's audiences as *different* from their own time. They lived under Elizabeth I, after all, a Tudor herself and the grand-daughter of the two characters united in this marriage, and thus ex-plicitly after the union of the two factions. Admittedly what is distant history to us was almost living memory to them: the equivalent of writing about World War I or the Spanish Flu today. But it was still historical, and not contemporary: the lessons to be drawn from it, if lessons there were, were not from immediate reference but from the same sort of echoes that we have examined above for the Roman plays. And so, of course, it is with us as well.

The American War of the Roses

At one level, the lessons I suggest we should draw from the partisanship of the War of the Roses cycle are similar to those we have already noted in the Roman plays. Once again we see political naïveté and an inability to adapt ushering in disaster: Henry VI is widely considered one of Shakespeare's weakest kings and it is largely because he continues acting as if the way he appeased his individual counselors at the start of *1 Henry VI* will work to mediate between partisan nobles in the later plays. He is not spectacularly successful in the first play that bears his name, but there is a hope there that gradually seeps away as he finds himself further and further out of step with the times. It is not quite that he, like Brutus, thinks of himself as living in the time of his forefathers but rather that he misses the very real transformation of English politics within his own reign. He was never a canny political operator, but even his baseline competence drains out as time goes by, through the hole created by his naïve belief that things are as they were before.

To a lesser extent, we might say the same about his chief rival, Richard, Duke of York. York is capable of playing the factional game—it nearly propels him to the crown and does crown two of his sons—but while he understands his own faction he is less skilled at recognizing how the opposing faction will respond. More than once he accepts King Henry's offers of peace or surrender only to be shocked when Queen Margaret and her allies refuse to stand down. This would not—or at least should not—surprise us as Americans after the 2020 election, which saw different parts of the Republican party accept and reject election results at different times and for different reasons (as well as one common reason, Donald Trump). But it is a shock to Richard because he still expects his opponents to follow the king, the ostensible leader of their country, *even while he himself refuses to do so.* It is not quite the same folly that Henry shows, but it is not for nothing that Richard too finds himself captured by the opposing side: both of them make assumptions about the way politics in their world works based on past, pre-factional experience, and it leads both of them astray.

But beyond the twin questions of political naïveté and adaptability, the three *Henry VI* plays and *Richard III* remind us of the sheer danger of partisan polarization in a way that the Roman plays do not. To be sure, Cinna the Poet might disagree, since the Roman mob tore him apart, but the scenes of partisan violence—and particularly the violence inspired but not formally sanctioned by the parties—in the War of the Roses cycle are more intense. The chief of these is Cade's rebellion (though arguably Richard III's various murders come in a close second).

Cade's rebellion in *2 Henry VI* is like Antony's riotous mob writ large. Instead of a single short scene, it takes over much of the action of one of the plays, and (unlike the plebeians in *Julius Caesar*) the mob has its own leader to push it forward and not just one extremely effective speech by Antony. Jack Cade is a quintessential conman, putting himself forward as a claimant to the throne even while his lower-class audience knows that he was born among them (4.1.33–65) and freely switching up both his self-justifications and his goals as he goes along. His rebellion results in vicious slaughter and the horrific image of two heads on pikes being paraded through the streets of London and made to kiss at the street corners. It is a visceral spectacle of the dangers of civil war—and because it is directly stirred up by Richard of York in support of his own claim to the throne, a deadly reminder of the dangers of partisan factionalism as well.

In American terms, we might wish to consider Trump a Cade figure, as Greenblatt strongly implies in his *Tyrant*,[15] were it not that (as we have discussed above) Shakespearean relevance is rarely so straight-forward or direct. Cade is a blowhard who lies about how he will be in charge to an audience that knows he lies and still eggs him on, but the parallels beyond that are extremely inexact: Trump, after all, was president for four years and Cade has nothing like that on his resume. Cade is not Trump, and none of Alexander Iden (who kills Cade), Henry VI, or Richard of York are Joe Biden.

Rather, Cade's rebellion should serve as a reminder that partisan polarization and the desire to do harm to the "other side" no matter the means frequently spiral out of control: sometimes to ends that the instigators wished for but could not cause directly themselves, and sometimes to places that they would be horrified by. Aggrieved, violent partisanship is not a housecat to be petted and made much of, but a tiger on whose back there is no safe handhold.

We have already had previews of this kind of political violence in America. The mob that stormed the US Capitol on January 6, 2021 did not hang Mike Pence, as they chanted they would, but it was not for lack of trying—or for lack of a makeshift gallows on which to do it. And while Trump and the other speakers at the rally at the Ellipse did not make quite the kind of direct calls for violence that Cade makes, the link between a particular set of political outcomes and the violence of that day was unmistakable. Likewise, of course, not Cade himself but Richard of York set in motion the forces that Cade leads, and while Cade comes to an unhappy and relatively anticlimactic end in a garden outside London, York comes much closer to the throne, literally sitting on it in *3 Henry VI* (1.1.50). This kind of politically associated violence is a natural outcome of this partisan polarization not because there is some unconscious social momentum that brings it about but because, in both America and medieval England, there are always unscrupulous in-dividuals who see that violence as a means to their own end—and who are willing to collaborate with each other to induce it and direct it.

Nor is Cade's rebellion the only reminder in the English history plays of the deadliness of this kind of partisanship. Richard of Gloucester, on his way to becoming Richard III, kills both through and around the law, having the Queen's brothers and Lord Hastings executed under color of law while his nephews in the Tower of London are assassinated—and he does the same for Henry VI personally. Nor is Richard the only one to stoop to murder and politically motivated execution, though he is the one most willing to get his hands dirty. Edward IV knows full well how his rival king came to die, but there is no question of prosecuting Richard for the murder: his partisan af-filiation is much more important than the crime.

We have not come to such a pass in America, or perhaps not yet. There have been political assassinations here, of course—1968 comes to mind repeatedly—but the present partisan polarization has not come to the level of seeing someone like Hillary Clinton, Barack Obama, or Donald Trump sentenced to death under color of law (nor even yet arrested, despite Trump's ongoing legal troubles with the United States and the state of New York and his own supporter's chants about Hillary urging him to "lock her up"). Yet while the specific details are not translatable, and we should not expect them to be, the overall sense of increasing danger from our polarized politics should not be ignored. The rise of so-called "stochastic" political violence—violence whose details are unpredictable, but whose overall statistical likelihood is undeniable[16]—should warn us that the differences here are of degree, and not kind. Just as we cannot be naïve about the degree of partisan polarization in America, and we cannot fail to adapt to it, we also cannot discount the dangers that it brings.

Joe Biden's America is not Marc Antony's Rome or Richard III's England. But the lessons of the partisanship we see in Shakespeare's plays about those other times and places should give us pause. While we should not necessarily look for the details of that drama to play itself out across our country, the broader point that we must be aware of and responsive to our own particular historical situation and its potential disasters cannot be ignored. This may seem like an obvious point but, as Shakespeare's plays show us, it is frequently overlooked. All too often, people look at their political moment and think "this isn't us" or "this can't be happening." But Shakespeare reminds us that denial will not work: we cannot afford to be Caesar or Henry VI, believing that everything will be fine if we just wish the problem away. We must be clearheaded and honest when looking at our own time, even and especially when that might show us things we do not wish to see.

Notes

1 All citations to the plays are from *The Complete Oxford Shakespeare*, ed. Stanley Wells and Gary Taylor (Oxford: Oxford University Press, 1987).
2 Michael Platt, *Rome and Romans According to Shakespeare* (Salzburg: Institut Für Englische Sprache Und Literatur, 1976), 187.
3 *Julius Caesar* 1.1.37, 42, 51, 1.3.125, 152, 3.2.186; *Antony and Cleopatra* 1.4.54, 3.5.18, 3.7.32, and the entire Sextus Pompey interlude.
4 For more on political friendship in the period, see Philip Goldfarb Styrt, *Shakespeare's Political Imagination: The Historicism of Setting* (London: Bloomsbury/Arden Shakespeare, 2021), 77–100; Tom MacFaul, *Male Friendship in Shakespeare and His Contemporaries*, (Cambridge: Cambridge

University Press, 2007), 117, 140; Jonathan Shelley, "'To seek new friends and stranger companies': The Expansion of Friendship in Early Modern England" (Ph. D. Dissertation, University of California at Berkeley, 2018), 39.

5 For excellent analyses of how this production cast Caesar as Trump, see Jeffrey Wilson, *Shakespeare and Trump* (Philadelphia: Temple University Press, 2020), 132ff., and Schapiro, *Divided*, 205ff.

6 "Trump: I alone can fix the system," *CNBC*, July 21, 2016 (https://www.cnbc.com/video/2016/07/21/trump-i-alone-can-fix-the-system.html).

7 Wilson, *Trump*, 53; Scott L. Newstok and Harry Berger, Jr., "Harrying after VV," in *Shakespeare After 9/11: How a Social Trauma Reshapes Interpretation, Shakespeare Yearbook* 20, ed. Douglas A. Brooks, Matthew Biberman, and Julia Reinhard Lupton (Lewiston: Edwin Mellen, 2011), 144.

8 Yu Jin Ko, "Donald Trump: Shakespeare's Lord of Misrule," in *Trump and Political Philosophy: Leadership, Statesmanship, and Tyranny*, ed. Angel Jaramillo Torres and Marc Benjamin Sable, pp. 149–62 (New York: Palgrave Macmillan, 2018), 159.

9 Goldfarb Styrt, *Political Imagination,* 29–30.

10 Alex Thompson and Theodoric Meyer, "Why Biden thinks the GOP fever could break (really)," *West Wing Playbook*, Politico, December 15, 2020 (https://www.politico.com/newsletters/transition-playbook/2020/12/15/why-biden-thinks-the-gop-fever-could-break-really-792320); Andrew Solender, "Biden Maintains Call for Bipartisanship Despite Likely Senate Majority," *Forbes*, January 6, 2021 (https://www.forbes.com/sites/andrewsolender/2021/01/06/biden-maintains-call-for-bipartisanship-despite-likely-senate-majority/?sh=44b7bc6f3b5a).

11 Steve Benen, "Republican leader envisions 'a 100-year majority'," *MSNBC*, November 6, 2014 (https://www.msnbc.com/rachel-maddow-show/republican-leader-envisions-100-year-majority-msna452886); Thomas B. Edsall, "Permanent Democratic Majority: New Study Says Yes," *Huffington Post*, May 14, 2009 (https://www.huffpost.com/entry/pemanent-democratic-major_n_186257).

12 James Pogue, "Inside the New Right, Where Peter Thiel Is Placing His Biggest Bets," *Vanity Fair*, April 20, 2022 (https://www.vanityfair.com/news/2022/04/inside-the-new-right-where-peter-thiel-is-placing-his-biggest-bets).

13 Brian Walsh, *Shakespeare, the Queen's Men, and the Elizabethan Performance of History* (Cambridge: Cambridge University Press, 2009), 119.

14 Stephen Greenblatt, *Tyrant: Shakespeare on Politics* (New York: WW Norton, 2018), 24–6.

15 Greenblatt, *Tyrant*, 41.

16 Jonathon Keats, "Jargon Watch: The Rising Danger of Stochastic Terrorism," *Wired*, January 21, 2019 (https://www.wired.com/story/jargon-watch-rising-danger-stochastic-terrorism/).

References

Benen, Steve. "Republican Leader Envisions 'a 100-year majority'." *MSNBC*, November 6, 2014 (https://www.msnbc.com/rachel-maddow-show/republican-leader-envisions-100-year-majority-msna452886).

Goldfarb Styrt, Philip. *Shakespeare's Political Imagination: The Historicism of Setting*. London: Bloomsbury/Arden Shakespeare, 2021.

Greenblatt, Stephen. *Tyrant: Shakespeare on Politics*. New York: WW Norton, 2018.

Keats, Jonathon. "Jargon Watch: The Rising Danger of Stochastic Terrorism." *Wired*, January 21, 2019 (https://www.wired.com/story/jargon-watch-rising-danger-stochastic-terrorism/).

Ko, Yu Jin. "Donald Trump: Shakespeare's Lord of Misrule," In *Trump and Political Philosophy: Leadership, Statesmanship, and Tyranny*, edited by Angel Jaramillo Torres and Marc Benjamin Sable, pp. 149–162. New York: Palgrave Macmillan, 2018.

MacFaul, Tom. *Male Friendship in Shakespeare and His Contemporaries*. Cambridge University Press, 2007.

Newstok, Scott L. and Harry Berger, Jr., "Harrying after VV," in *Shakespeare After 9/11: How a Social Trauma Reshapes Interpretation*, Shakespeare Yearbook 20, edited by Douglas A. Brooks, Matthew Biberman, and Julia Reinhard Lupton, pp. 141–152. Lewiston: Edwin Mellen, 2011.

Platt, Michael. *Rome and Romans According to Shakespeare*. Salzburg: Institut Für Englische Sprache Und Literatur, 1976.

Pogue, James. "Inside the New Right, Where Peter Thiel Is Placing His Biggest Bets." *Vanity Fair*, April 20, 2022 (https://www.vanityfair.com/news/2022/04/inside-the-new-right-where-peter-thiel-is-placing-his-biggest-bets).

Schapiro, James. *Shakespeare in a Divided America*. New York: Penguin Press, 2020.

Shakespeare, William. *The Complete Oxford Shakespeare*, edited by Stanley Wells and Gary Taylor. Oxford: Oxford University Press, 1987.

Shelley, Jonathan. "'To Seek New Friends and Stranger Companies': The Expansion of Friendship in Early Modern England." Ph. D. Dissertation, University of California at Berkeley, 2018.

Solender, Andrew. "Biden Maintains Call for Bipartisanship Despite Likely Senate Majority." *Forbes*, January 6, 2021 (https://www.forbes.com/sites/andrewsolender/2021/01/06/biden-maintains-call-for-bipartisanship-despite-likely-senate-majority/?sh=44b7bc6f3b5a).

Thompson, Alex and Theodoric Meyer. "Why Biden thinks the GOP fever could break (really)." *West Wing Playbook*, Politico, December 15, 2020 (https://www.politico.com/newsletters/transition-playbook/2020/12/15/why-biden-thinks-the-gop-fever-could-break-really-792320).

"Trump: I Alone Can Fix the System," *CNBC*, July 21, 2016 (https://www.cnbc.com/video/2016/07/21/trump-i-alone-can-fix-the-system.html).

Walsh, Brian. *Shakespeare, the Queen's Men, and the Elizabethan Performance of History*. Cambridge: Cambridge University Press, 2009.

Wilson, Jeffrey. *Shakespeare and Trump*. Philadelphia: Temple University Press, 2020.

2 Pretextual Insurrections and Unpunished Crimes

The attempted insurrection at the US Capitol on January 6, 2021, went beyond mere partisan polarization, so the Big Lie of the stolen 2020 election is not merely another symptom of deepening partisan divides within America. It is its own phenomenon, connected to but not the same as the factionalism we looked at in the previous chapter. But like those partisan divides, Shakespeare once again has something to say about it. As always, of course, we cannot simply equate Shakespeare's characters and our modern politicians. But the January 6 insurrection should nevertheless draw our attention to three Shakespeare plays in particular: *Richard II*, for its treatment of something like the Big Lie in Bolingbroke's claims that he has returned to England only to receive his father's inheritance; *Coriolanus*, for its depiction of a disputed election and its consequences; and *Much Ado About Nothing*, for what happens when sedition is not punished.

Even if Elizabeth I thought she was Richard II, Joe Biden is definitely not, nor is Donald Trump Henry Bolingbroke. Likewise, neither of them is Coriolanus or either Aragonese prince in *Much Ado*. But the lessons for our time we can and should draw from Shakespeare are still rooted in understanding how each of these particular situations resolves itself—as long as we remember to pay attention to the specifics of each set of circumstances, both in the plays and in our own world. Once we do that, we can see that Shakespeare was concerned about the destabilizing effects of attacks on authority that are not recognized as such: of those who pretend a plot against the state is patriotism, those who claim to be only going through the legal process while contemplating the overthrow of the very system that process relies on, and those who wilfully ignore the peril that the state is in.

DOI: 10.4324/9781003331391-3

Henry Bolingbroke's inheritance and Richard II's throne

Richard II was not a good king, and Shakespeare's play does not do him any favors. *Richard II* begins with the exile of Henry Bolingbroke, the future Henry IV, as a result of a dispute with Thomas Mowbray, Duke of Norfolk, over the latter's role in the death of Duke of Gloucester, uncle to both Richard and Henry. Historically—and there are implications of this in the play as well—it was strongly suspected that Mowbray did what he did because Richard wanted him to. As a result, the exile of both Mowbray and Henry, which is imposed by Richard to prevent a trial by combat, can be seen as self-serving on Richard's part: a way to avoid the truth coming to light.[1] It makes Richard, who had previously agreed to the trial, seem at best weak and at worst conniving. The second impression is reinforced when Richard takes advantage of Henry's exile to seize the estates the latter should have inherited when his father, John of Gaunt, dies. Richard is not acting like a king, and he does not come off well in his exchanges with Gaunt before the man's death—exchanges which include a famous speech by Gaunt in which he extols the virtues of England and laments Richard's failure to live up to the crown (2.1.31–68).

This all might tend to make us sympathetic to Henry when he returns to England before the time of his exile is complete, insisting that he is only violating the royal decree in order to claim what is legally owed to him: his inheritance. Richard has clearly done Henry wrong, at least with his inheritance and (it seems likely) with the exile itself as well. It would seem, therefore, that we ought to think well of Henry, as indeed the common people of England do upon his return.

But if the play makes it clear that Richard is a bad king who has treated Henry badly, it also makes it clear that Henry is lying when he says he has come back only for his own right to the duchy of Lancaster. He is clearly preparing to overthrow Richard—and this is a crucial distinction. Richard is at best a mediocre monarch, but he is the rightful king, and that means that Henry's rebellion is illegitimate. There is never really any question of this. In fact, it is precisely because any rebellion would be illegitimate that Henry continues to put forward the false claim that he has returned only for his inheritance long past the point at which the assertion is laughable (3.3.194). As with all treason, Henry's course of action is illegitimate until it is legitimized, and since it can only be legitimized by overthrowing the reigning king it cannot be acknowledged until the king is actually overthrown.

Richard makes this process very uncomfortable for Henry precisely because he lampshades the absurdity of it all, turning the very solemn process Henry has planned to make it look as if Richard is voluntarily resigning his throne into a clear and public scene of a forced deposition. Henry still becomes king. But because of Richard's intransigent insistence on showing it for what it is, and not for what Henry wishes it to seem, he cannot do so legitimately. It was this deposition of Richard II, heir of Edward III, that ultimately brought about the Wars of the Roses as the *other* great-grandsons and great-great-grandsons and so forth of Edward III fought over who could most legitimately claim the throne in his absence. In other words, the way in which Henry IV deposed Richard II ultimately led to all the partisan polarization between the white rose and the red that we have already examined. Because Henry's gambit only works to put him on the throne, not to make him the true and legitimate heir, the system ends up falling apart.

This is the true danger of Henry's approach. It is not, like Cade's rebellion, a piecemeal attack on the houses of state doomed to fail; nor is it, like Edward IV's brutal warfare against Henry VI, an outright bloody fight for the throne. It is treason and sedition couched in the language of law and order, and that paradoxically makes it more corrosive than anything Cade or Edward does. Because Henry claims until the last possible moment not to be doing precisely what he is doing, he sets himself and the system up for further failures of the same kind: first the rebellions put down in the two Henry IV plays, and then Richard of York's more successful parliamentary maneuvers in *2 Henry VI*. Henry creates a situation in which there is the color of law over a fundamentally lawless action, and this situation replicates itself again and again, ultimately destroying the very system that he wished to rule.

1399 and 2021

The parallels between Henry Bolingbroke's rebellion and Donald Trump's incitement of insurrection on January 6, 2021, are hardly direct. It would be trivial to list distinctions: Trump, first of all, was legally president at the time of his actions while Bolingbroke was not a king (though the federal judiciary has needed to remind him that "presidents are not kings" either).[2] Even more importantly, Bolingbroke succeeded and Trump failed; Henry IV reigned for 14 years while Donald Trump ceded the presidency a mere 14 *days* after the insurrection.

But as we have seen, Shakespearean parallels are not and should not be as simple as that. We can see Bolingbroke's behavior in its historical and theatrical context and recognize in it the same sense as we see in contemporary politics: the corrosive idea that a facially plausible excuse should be allowed to smooth over what everyone knows is an illegitimate action, and that those who object to the illegitimate action are acting hysterically—right up until they are proven right.

It is not only the actual insurrection of January 6 that demonstrates this element of Trumpian politics. Perhaps the first highly public example was the so-called Muslim ban, which Trump called for in so many words on the campaign trail and then went about implementing as soon as he took office. A majority of the US Supreme Court ruled that, despite Candidate Trump proposing an unconstitutional religious test for immigration, and despite President Trump openly acknowledging that the way it was implemented (via selected country bans) was intended as a direct replacement for that, the candidate's statements could not be taken as any evidence whatsoever of the ban's intent or effect.[3] Much like fourteenth-century Englishmen in Shakespeare's play are asked to believe that Henry Bolingbroke is not back in England for the crown, Americans were asked to simply pretend that the State Department travel ban was somehow wholly segregated from what Trump had discussed on the campaign trail.

The same process worked itself out time and again in the courts throughout the Trump administration: the evidence of what was said and done would contradict the official legal line of the administration and yet the Justice Department and sometimes the courts themselves would insist that none of it mattered. In several cases, the evidence of reality did eventually discredit the administration's claims: when emails were found showing that Wilbur Ross, the Commerce Secretary, had fabricated the justification for omitting undocumented immigrants from the census, the rule was defeated in court.[4] Similarly, the ridiculous claim that by *failing* to repeal the Affordable Care Act and only lowering the penalty for being uninsured to zero dollars Congress had somehow demonstrated a belief that the entire Affordable Care Act should be overturned was eventually rejected—though it took a narrow decision at the Supreme Court to do so.[5] But this was not always the case. And in some instances, the plausible falsehoods became larger than the court system alone could refute, even when Trump lost.

The classic example of this is, of course, the Big Lie itself, the claims about the stolen 2020 election that led to the insurrection. But the similar issue of Trump's involvement with Russia in the *2016* election was the proving ground for those same techniques. Multiple people involved in Trump's campaign, including his campaign manager, were convicted of various crimes connected to cooperating with Russia,[6] but his dominant message remained "No Collusion" (which, since it is not a legal term, was not subject to being legally disproved). Even more blatantly, Trump said on live television during the campaign that he wanted Russia to help him by finding and releasing emails of Hillary Clinton's.[7] Yet the claim was nevertheless made that even suggesting Trump or his campaign thought about talking to Russia in any way was the greatest unfairness on Earth.[8]

But this is a book about Shakespeare and Biden, not Shakespeare and Trump, so it is the Big Lie and the January 6 insurrection—both of which remain, astoundingly, live issues in American politics—that most concern us here. Both of these are frequently treated, from the right, as if they were genuine, good-faith efforts to better the US electoral process.[9] This might once have seemed plausible when it comes to the Big Lie, though the repeated failure to produce any actual evidence of large-scale or significant voter fraud calls that into question.[10] But it becomes ridiculous when the same thought process is applied to the January 6 insurrection. Just as Bolingbroke might, just possibly, have actually wanted to receive his inheritance from John of Gaunt and then return to his exile, it is theoretically possible that Republican lawmakers and right-wing pundits have a burning desire to understand and combat any form of illegitimate voting but would be willing to accept Joe Biden's win after some (unspecified) standard of proof was met. However, the claim that violently storming the Capitol to prevent Congress from counting electoral votes, interrupting the process, and causing members of Congress to flee falls under the same exemption is ridiculous—just as the claim would be that Henry imprisoned Richard and brought him to the place where he would surrender the crown solely out of concern for his own inheritance.

But of course, Henry did not make that claim. By the time he had actually imprisoned the king, he had made clear to all that his ambitions were not nearly so small. And the same is true, if we look carefully, of today's Republican party.

The House of Representatives' special committee on January 6 and the Justice Department investigations into the insurrection are still ongoing as I write this, and the details of all their findings are therefore not yet known. But much has already been revealed, first in public before the insurrection itself took place and since then through the drips and drops of various "tell-all" books, Congressional leaks, press releases, and legal filings. And what these revelations show is that Trump and his allies were just as clear about their goals to themselves and their foot soldiers as the future Henry IV was to his. Everyone knew what was going on.[11]

This applies to both active insurrectionists and those who planned the coup. Before January 6, Trump's advisors put together a gameplan for overturning the election—that is, for a coup.[12] At the same time, right-wing paramilitaries planned to do the same by violence, while other rioters explicitly thought of themselves part of a "revolution."[13] Numerous rioters have been indicted for crimes up to and including seditious conspiracy as a result of their attempts to stop the electoral vote count, and some have already been convicted or pled guilty.[14] Trump has openly stated that he wished Pence to overturn the election, and told the crowd to march towards the Capitol during the January 6 rally that preceded the attack. And Congressman Mo Brooks alleges he has continued to pursue overturning the election result even afterwards.[15]

All of this has led pundits, the January 6 committee, and a federal district court to suggest that Trump himself committed and could be legally liable for crimes involved in the insurrection.[16] The liability suggested so far does not rise to treason or sedition but includes obstruction, conspiracy, and fraud. All of these were in the service of the seditious purpose of seizing power. Like Henry Bolingbroke was never convicted of treason, it is unlikely that Trump will ever be held legally accountable for these actions. But he, like the others, was perfectly well aware of what was going on, and why.

The degree of Trump's involvement has become clearer over time. Just weeks after the attack, Trump explicitly stated that the vice-president should have "overturned" the election.[17] He also pledged to pardon those involved in the insurrection, if re-elected.[18] At the same time, it has been discovered that Trump's advisors drafted, and Trump looked over, an executive order that would have had the military seize voting machines in key states.[19] In other words, we now know that Trump not only supported plans to overturn the election but was involved in those plans and now has signaled to the insurrectionists that he will shield them from consequences if he can.

And it is not just Trump. The Republican party has rallied around the contradictory ideas that it was all exaggerated nothings and that the insurrectionists were right and it was necessary.[20] As Biden himself said on the anniversary of the January 6 insurrection, Trump and his supporters engaged in a long-term struggle to "rewrite history" to make it seem as if the November 6, 2020 elections were the illegitimate attempt to gain power and the January 6 insurrection was the heroic work of restoring the people's will.[21] A fundamentally similar process was at work in Shakespeare's medieval England, as we see in the plays that come after *Richard II*. The two parts of *Henry IV* and *Henry V* are both intimately concerned with re-legitimizing the act of treason with which Henry IV's reign began, and thereby rewriting history to make the overthrow of the king seem righteous. At Agincourt, Henry V gives a brief list of all that they did, focusing on the plea (to God, if not to voters, since he was an absolute monarch) to "think not upon the fault my father made/In compassing the crown" (4.1.290–1). As with the sleight of hand Trump and his supporters now engage in, Henry wishes to obscure and hide who is at fault. And while we do not know the ultimate consequences of Trump's Big Lie, we do know the consequences of Henry IV's, as Shakespeare dramatized them: two more rounds of civil war over six plays[22] and thousands of wasteful deaths. Even though Henry IV's coup was bloodless in the moment (Richard II is not killed until a full act later), the dangers of a pretextual insurrection echo down Shakespeare's collected works.

There are obvious differences between the two Henry's situation and Trump's, not least of which is that Biden, and not Trump, is currently president. We cannot and should not take them to be perfect mirror images of each other. But the fundamental message of Shakespeare's plays is nevertheless relevant to our current situation. Henry Bolingbroke's rebellion broke Shakespeare's medieval England. Even if we accept the strongest version of his right to return to claim his inheritance despite his banishment, we cannot ignore that it is fundamentally a pretext for the rebellion. The same is true of the January 6 insurrection. Even if we suspect the existence of widespread voter fraud (which remains not only unproven but disproven—hence the term the Big Lie), we cannot ignore that the claims surrounding it are and have always been a pretext for a coup: either in 2020 or as practice for 2024.[23] An important sign of this is that those cases of voter fraud that have been uncovered have been both minor (individuals, not systematic fraud) and often pro-Trump.[24] Similarly, attempts to breach voting machine security have come from pro-Trump sources.[25] Just as Henry IV's triumphant procession through England and his massing of armies in *Richard II* gave the lie to his claim that all he wanted was his own inheritance, Trump's lack of attention to actual details of voting procedure and fraud reveals that his Big Lie is just as much of a pretext for sedition as Bolingbroke's was for treason.

No matter the pretext, Shakespeare's plays teach us that ignoring sedition and treason is fundamentally harmful to the state. It is no accident that so many of Shakespeare's plays, from the English history plays here to the Roman tragedies of the previous chapter and beyond, are concerned with what happens when the transition of power in a state goes wrong. Whatever imagined justification there may be for it, I argue that Shakespeare shows us the deep danger of allowing a pretext to blind us to sedition.

Elections, disputes, and danger to the state

There is, of course, another option here to consider. Rather than describing the Big Lie and the January 6 insurrection as Bolingbroke-style sedition and treason, we could also view them as violent resistance to an unpopular electoral result. After all, the president is an elected official, not a king. And it turns out Shakespeare has something to say about that too, through one of his Roman plays: *Coriolanus*.

Near the heart of *Coriolanus* is a disputed election where the loser declares himself legitimately elected to the highest office of the land and announces that any attempt to prevent him from taking office is illegitimate. The title character, Caius Martius Coriolanus, stood for election as consul, and indeed appeared to have received the votes of the people to claim it. But after Coriolanus leaves the stage, the tribunes of the people, two other office-holders whose role is to vet and declare the people's choice to the assembled Senate, come onstage and, in a dramatic scene, convince the voters to "revoke/Your ignorant election" (2.3.218–9).

Coriolanus arrives at the Capitol expecting to hear himself declared consul and is instead confronted with the grinning tribunes, who announce that he is not (3.1). He is apoplectic. Over the course of the following act he repeatedly confronts the tribunes over it and ultimately things grow to such a head that the people riot. Coriolanus is saved from their immediate wrath but condemned as a traitor, and he is exiled from Rome entirely.

We might, through a distorted mirror, recognize this as a version of our own political situation in late 2020 and 2021. An election that one of the parties claims was changed overnight while no one was looking; an unpopular politician who many people think won the election; a formal ratification of that vote that turns out differently than expected; a mob of enraged citizens calling for a politician's blood and only being stopped by the narrowest of margins. All of these are parallel elements, and we might be inclined to draw those parallels closely.

As I have suggested before, however, this kind of overly direct parallelism does a disservice to the complexity and nuance both of Shakespeare and of reality. The difference here matters. Most notably, the mob in Shakespeare opposes the defeated candidate, Coriolanus, unlike the January 6 insurrectionists who supported Trump, while it is the political elites, the senators, who believe Coriolanus has won the election, and Trump's supporters consistently claim that the elites oppose him. There are also vital differences in how the election happened (*Coriolanus* has no actual formal balloting of votes) and what the consequences of it are (Trump has not, as of this writing, been banished from ever setting foot in America upon pain of death).

What, then, can we get from a more robust way of thinking about these differences and the Shakespearean situation? I suggest that the dominant theme of the play is that of the difficulty of grasping political change: much like the Roman plays we encountered in the previous chapter, *Coriolanus* is focused on what it is like when the political rules you thought you were playing by are no longer applicable. Coriolanus fails (to his death) because he cannot adapt to the changing political climate of Rome, most of all the creation of the tribunes. The tribunes, however, also have their own problems adapting to the world they occupy. By banishing Coriolanus, they create a threat that almost destroys Rome. The banished Coriolanus joins their arch-enemies, the Volsces, and leads an army back to burn Rome—and this is clearly marked in the play as the tribunes' fault (4.6.92–168). Just like Coriolanus, the tribunes are too self-assured about their understanding of Roman politics, and while they do not die like he does the play is equally clear that they screwed up.

As a result, I suggest that *Coriolanus* teaches us two things. One is that, in our current political moment, we must not cling too fiercely to our belief in the invulnerability of American institutions. Much as in the previous chapter, I suggest that this means we need to be realistic about the changing political climate and not see current political trends through rose-colored glasses. Democracy itself does not vote, does not pass laws, and does not prevent calamities. Only what we do with democracy does that; we cannot assume that the institutions we know and love are self-defending or self-instituting. Just as in the discussion of the other Roman plays, then, I suggest that *Coriolanus* tells us that we cannot be complacent about the unchanging nature of the American political system.

But the *Coriolanus* connection goes further than that. It is a message of caution—not a call for inaction, but for caution about assuming that our own knee-jerk responses are the correct ones. Both Coriolanus and the tribunes seize the moment aggressively, or try to; both create disasters by doing so. This does not necessarily mean that there is nothing either of them could do—or therefore nothing we can do—that would have worked out better. But it does mean that we must be certain of the road forward not because the thoughts we have about it align with our preconceived notions, but because we have actually considered the future. We probably do not want to be too much like Aufidius, general of the Volsces, given that history tells us the Romans overwhelmed them rather quickly. But it is worth remembering in this play that it is Rome's enemy who actually plans for the situation he faces—and who comes out of the play strengthened by Rome's losses.

The importance of consequences

If *Coriolanus* is a call to caution, we must avoid confusing that with a lack of consequences. Being certain about what to do, or trying to be, does not mean ignoring bad deeds. We have seen that in our society with the legacy of torture under George W. Bush: failing to prosecute crimes is not itself a healing act, and the Republican party did not suddenly join hands with Barack Obama in bipartisan splendor because he refrained from charging Bush-era officials with war crimes. We see this in a more explicit shape in Shakespeare's *Much Ado About Nothing*, which starts and ends with two punishments of Don John, its villain: the first too light, and the second unclear.

The play begins in the immediate aftermath of a quashed revolt. Don John, bastard brother to Don Pedro the prince, has been apprehended and brought back to face judgment. Or at least so it seems at first. But in fact, the judgment has already been given, and it is an exceptionally lenient one—or perhaps it would be more accurate to say that judgment has been avoided entirely. Don John is a rebel and a traitor, and Claudio's new honors at the start of the play are specifically granted for defeating him (1.3.61–2). But he is also restored already to something very like his former position. He is not imprisoned. He is not, as far as we can tell, punished, except insofar as the very idea of acknowledging his brother's authority is something he feels as a punishment. He hates being reconciled with his brother, but despite his distaste for it, he has been forgiven (1.3.25–6, 20–1). In other words, there have been no consequences for his defiance of his brother—even though that defiance led to an active war that has just been resolved.

We should not, by the way, undersell the seriousness of this war, for all that few men died in it (1.1.7). There is no reason to suspect that few dead on one side means few dead on the other; it could well be a situation like Henry V's battle at Agincourt where the lack of casualties was in direct proportion to the victory (*Henry V* 4.8.80–106). In addition, the play itself goes to great pains to alert us to the fact that Don Pedro and his allies *expected* casualties even if they were fortunate or skilled enough not to have many. Beatrice asks how many men Benedick killed, and while she is clearly mocking him, the mockery comes from the idea that he himself would fail to kill people in battle, not from the idea that there would be no opportunity to do so (1.1.40–43). Claudio, for his part, is lionized (literally, he did "in the figure of a lamb the feats of a lion" [1.1.14–5]) for his valor in combat, and describes that combat having driven out thoughts of love from his mind before battle (1.1.282). Benedick himself describes the seriousness of Claudio's warlike mind in the campaign (2.3.12–20)—and again, the fact that he does so to belittle his friend's more lovesick attitude during the play does not undo his prior military frame of mind. The war that has just ended was a real war, even if it was spectacularly successful, and the threat Don John posed was equally real even if he lost conclusively.

As such, it is remarkable that Don John has been taken back into his brother's trust so quickly, and indeed Leonato literally remarks on its recency (1.1.147–9). We in the audience, in turn, discover that Don John has not reformed in the least. He still wishes to do nothing but ill to his brother and his friends (1.3.62–3). And Don John does not hide this from others: before the successful trick he pulls to divide Claudio and Hero, he tries another that ends up only creating a few moments of awkwardness (2.1.145–161). This foreshadowing of his larger, more successful plan to cause mischief should have been a warning (if his rebellion was not) that he did not have Claudio's or Don Pedro's best interest at heart.

And yet Don Pedro's excessive forbearance towards his brother continues despite all evidence. Not only does he replant Don John in his grace and trust, he acts upon that planting as well, allowing his brother to convince him (and Claudio) of Hero's infidelity—and worse, to dictate the means by which they will investigate his claim (3.2.72–124). It is perhaps defensible, in the interest of harmony, that Don Pedro and Claudio listen to Don John's accusation. But when they go further, taking Don John's suggested means for investigation, they make a near-fatal mistake—much the same mistake, indeed, that Shakespeare's Othello makes when he listens to Iago and not Desdemona. We can see here the excess of trust that Don Pedro extends to his treasonous brother. He hands over a vital question of political and social alliance—whether the marriage of Hero and Claudio will go forward—over to a man who was until literally a few days ago engaged in active war against him.

Like the significance of Don John's treason, the stakes of the Hero-Claudio marriage are also sometimes overlooked. By arranging the marriage of these two, Don Pedro is bringing one of his favored and best soldiers formally into the Spanish fold by marrying him to the daughter of a Spanish governor, making a political alliance out of a personal connection. Threatening this match, therefore, is political dynamite. Don Pedro does need to investigate Don John's claim—if Hero cuckolds Claudio, that would be its own crisis—but accusing

Hero directly is a massive step. We see just how massive in her father Leonato's reaction to the suggestion that the princes and Claudio might be wrong about Hero: a rant where he comes near to announcing an intention to rebel in his own right (4.1.193–202).

Doing this on the word and evidence of a known traitor is a sign of how excessive Don Pedro's unmerited faith in his brother is—and how few consequences Don John has actually suffered for his treason. Making it worse is the fact that we, the audience, already know that Don John has faked the scene he uses as evidence, and will receive even more detailed corroboration from the drunk Borachio immediately after. Thus we know for a fact that Don Pedro's faith is misplaced.

But I suggest that the larger lesson here is that while the audience knows that Don John is untrustworthy, *so should Don Pedro*. Don John was never trustworthy. There was no actual sign of remorse, reflection, or reformation on his part. Don Pedro simply glossed over his brother's rebellion and believed that by letting bygones be bygones all would be well. And this is dangerous.

It is no mistake that the happy ending of this play is joined to the flight and capture of Don John. The play ends with a dance, but the lines immediately before are darker: Don John is "brought with arméd men back to Messina," a strong contrast with his initial free return in his brother's company, and Benedick promises to "devise … brave punishments for him" (5.4.126, 127). Don John's renewed treachery *must* be dealt with for the ending to be happy. If he were still at large, or if Don Pedro were once again going to forgive his crimes without punishment, his shadow would still loom over the joy. Don John almost literally demands punishment. The marriage between Claudio and Hero is saved by Conrad and Borachio's drunkenness, the city watch's accidental competence, and Hero and the friar's plan to protect her. But simply because the worst has not happened does not mean that the man who tried to bring it about should be spared. Don Pedro already tried that with his brother's rebellion; perhaps it was because it was so easily put down with minimal casualties to his side that he was so lenient not just to Don Pedro but to his known associates like Conrad and Borachio. Now that his treachery has repeated itself, there is no remaining choice but to punish him.

Obviously the January 6 insurrection has very few direct parallels to Don John's meddling in Hero and Claudio's marriage. We could perhaps conjure some up: both relied on a staged form of a Big Lie with little concern for the underlying truth, for instance. But as I have repeatedly emphasized, we do not find the significance of Shakespeare to this political moment in simple equations between Shakespeare and society. Instead, we should look at the broader picture. *Much Ado About Nothing* is a play about how allowing someone to continue to strew lies and mischief even after you know they have bad intentions leads to great danger. Put that way, perhaps, it seems obvious. But it is not obvious to Don Pedro—and it is not always as obvious in our modern world as we might expect.

There has been much gnashing of teeth in the political press about whether we ought to prosecute former Trump administration officials, members of Congress, or Trump himself for their complicity or active engagement in the January 6 insurrection.[26] This is despite the fact that not only were they part of the attack on American democracy, but they also continue to make statements and take actions that show they hold the same beliefs and desire the same outcomes as they did on January 6, with little to no visible remorse. It is obvious that Don John should not be allowed to do whatever he wants in the wake of his rebellion—allowing him to do so nearly causes a breach between Aragon and Messina. We need not say that Trump is Don John or the Q-Anon shaman is Borachio to say that the same logic applies to those who already attacked the US Capitol once. Merrick Garland may or may not "devise brave punishments" for the January 6 insurrectionists—or those who organized the attack and gave it purpose—but I argue that *Much Ado About Nothing* shows us that such punishments are the appropriate response to unrepentant insurrection.

Notes

1 For more on this issue see Graham Holderness, Nick Potter, and John Turner, *Shakespeare: The Play of History* (Iowa City: University of Iowa Press, 1988), 25–32; Lukas Lammers, *Shakespearean Temporalities: History on the Early Modern Stage*, Routledge Studies in Shakespeare (New York: Routledge, 2018), 65–70.

2 Committee on the Judiciary, United State House of Representatives v. Donald F. McGhan II, Civ. No. 19-cv-2379, (DC District 2019), at 114 (https://ecf.dcd.uscourts.gov/cgi-bin/show_public_doc?2019cv2379-46); Donald J. Trump v. Bennie G. Thompson, Civil Action No. 21-cv-2769 (DC District 2021) at 18 (https://ecf.dcd.uscourts.gov/cgi-bin/show_public_doc?2021cv2769-35).

3 Trump v. Hawaii, 585 US___(2018) (https://www.supremecourt.gov/opinions/17pdf/17-965_h315.pdf).

4 Department of Commerce v. New York, 588 US___(2019) (https://www.supremecourt.gov/opinions/18pdf/18-966_bq7c.pdf).

5 California et al., v. Texas et al., 593 US___(2021) (https://www.supremecourt.gov/opinions/20pdf/19-840_6jfm.pdf).

6 "Factbox: Here are eight Trump associates arrested or convicted of crimes," *Reuters*, August 20, 2020 (https://www.reuters.com/article/us-usa-

trump-bannon-associates-factbox/factbox-here-are-eight-trump-associates-arrested-or-convicted-of-crimes-idUSKBN25G1YU).

7 "Donald Trump Asks Russia to Find Hillary Clinton's Emails," *C-SPAN*, July 27, 2016 (https://www.c-span.org/video/?c4615538/donald-trump-asks-russia-find-hillary-clintons-emails).

8 See among many Paolo Chavez and Benjamin Siegel, "Trump takes aim at Sessions for 'Russian Witch Hunt Hoax' in tweet," *ABC News*, June 5, 2018 (https://abcnews.go.com/Politics/trump-questions-delay-inspector-general-report-rivals-tweet/story?id=55655234).

9 Sam Metz, "GOP censures Cheney, Kinzinger as it assails Jan. 6 probe," *Associated Press*, February 4, 2022 (https://apnews.com/article/donald-trump-salt-lake-city-election-2020-campaign-2016-liz-cheney-cca6eba133 e2edee7987cac10e86d5c7).

10 Christina A. Cassidy and the Associated Press, "Investigation finds only 475 cases of potential voter fraud in battleground states won by Biden," *Fortune*, December 14, 2021 (https://fortune.com/2021/12/14/trump-voter-fraud-investigation-biden-battleground-states-only-475-potential-voter-fraud-cases/).

11 Josh Kovensky, "From Nov. 4 to Jan. 6, The MAGA Team Knew Exactly What They Were Doing," *TPM*, April 25, 2022 (https://talkingpointsmemo.com/muckraker/from-nov-4-to-jan-6-the-maga-team-knew-exactly-what-they-were-doing).

12 Jose Pagliery, "Trump Adviser Peter Navarro Lays Out How He and Bannon Planned to Overturn Biden's Electoral Win," *The Daily Beast*, December 28, 2021 (https://www.thedailybeast.com/trump-advisor-peter-navarro-lays-out-how-he-and-steve-bannon-planned-to-overturn-bidens-electoral-win); John McCormack, "John Eastman vs. the Eastman Memo," *The National Review*, October 22, 2021 (https://www.nationalreview.com/2021/10/john-eastman-vs-the-eastman-memo/).

13 Alan Feuer, "Document in Jan. 6 Case Shows Plan to Storm Government Buildings," *New York Times,* March 14, 2022 (https://www.nytimes.com/2022/03/14/us/politics/enrique-tarrio-jan-6-document.html); United States of America v. Brian Ulrich, 22-cr-15 (APM) (DC District); Ryan J. Reilly, "U.S. wants prison time for rioter who said she would 'absolutely' storm Capitol again," *NBC News*, March 16, 2022 (https://www.nbcnews.com/politics/justice-department/doj-wants-prison-time-rioter-said-absolutely-storm-capitol-rcna19970).

14 US Department of Justice, *Leader of Oath Keepers and 10 Other Individuals Indicted in Federal Court for Seditious Conspiracy and Other Offenses Related to U.S. Capitol Breach.* January 13, 2022 (https://www.justice.gov/opa/pr/leader-oath-keepers-and-10-other-individuals-indicted-federal-court-seditious-conspiracy-and); United States of America v. Guy Wesley Reffitt, 21-cr-32 (DLF) (DC District); United States v. William Todd Wilson, 22-cr-152 (APM) (DC District).

15 Mo Brooks, *Statement by Mo Brooks* (mobrooks.com/statement-by-mo-brooks/), accessed May 3, 2022.

16 Marcy Wheeler, "Finally, Everyone Is Talking About Trump's Obstruction on January 6," *Emptywheel*, December 14, 2021 (https://www.emptywheel.net/2021/12/14/finally-everyone-is-talking-about-trumps-obstruction-on-

january-6/); John C. Eastman v. Bennie G. Thompson, et al., 8:22-cv-00099-DOC-DFM (C.D. Cal. 2022).

17 Libby Cathey, "Trump suggests Pence should have 'overturned' 2020 election," *ABC News*, January 31, 2022 (https://abcnews.go.com/Politics/trump-suggests-pence-overturned-2020-election/story?id=82581412).

18 Ewan Palmer, "Donald Trump Doubles Down on Pardoning Jan. 6 Capitol Rioters, Says Many Not Guilty," *Newsweek*, February 2, 2022 (https://www.newsweek.com/trump-pardon-jan6-capitol-lindsey-graham-newsmax-1675289).

19 Hugo Lowell, "Revealed: Trump reviewed draft order that authorized voting machines to be seized," *The Guardian*, February 4, 2022 (https://www.theguardian.com/us-news/2022/feb/04/trump-draft-order-voting-machines-white-house-meeting).

20 Conor Friedersdorf, "The Contested Significance of January 6," *The Atlantic*, January 12, 2022 (https://www.theatlantic.com/ideas/archive/2022/01/the-contested-significance-of-january-6/621235).

21 Joseph Biden, *Remarks by President Biden to Mark One Year Since the January 6th Deadly Assault on the US Capitol.* January 6, 2022 (http://www.whitehouse.gov/briefing-room/speeches-remarks/2022/01/06/remarks-by-president-biden-to-mark-one-year-since-the-january-6th-deadly-assault-on-the-us-capitol/).

22 *1 & 2 Henry IV, 1, 2, & 3 Henry VI*, and *Richard III*.

23 J. Michael Luttig, "The Republican blueprint to steal the 2024 election," *CNN*, April 27, 2022 (https://www.cnn.com/2022/04/27/opinions/gop-blueprint-to-steal-the-2024-election-luttig/index.html).

24 Cassidy and Associated Press, "Investigation."

25 Alexandra Ulmer and Nathan Layne, "Trump allies breach U.S. voting systems in search of 2020 fraud 'evidence'," *Reuters*, April 28, 2022 (https://www.reuters.com/investigates/special-report/usa-election-breaches/).

26 Robert Anello, "Can the Capitol Insurrection Result In Prosecution of Members of Congress?" *Forbes*, September 13, 2021 (https://www.forbes.com/sites/insider/2021/09/13/prosecuting-lawmakers-in-connection-with-the-capitol-insurrection/?sh=68f5c8bd47c0)n

References

Anello, Robert. "Can the Capitol Insurrection Result In Prosecution of Members of Congress?" *Forbes*, September 13, 2021 (https://www.forbes.com/sites/insider/2021/09/13/prosecuting-lawmakers-in-connection-with-the-capitol-insurrection/?sh=68f5c8bd47c0)n.

Biden, Joseph. *Remarks by President Biden to Mark One Year Since the January 6th Deadly Assault on the US Capitol.* January 6, 2022 (http://www.whitehouse.gov/briefing-room/speeches-remarks/2022/01/06/remarks-by-president-biden-to-mark-one-year-since-the-january-6th-deadly-assault-on-the-us-capitol/).

Brooks, Mo. *Statement by Mo Brooks* (mobrooks.com/statement-by-mo-brooks/). Accessed May 3, 2022.

Cassidy, Christina A. and the Associated Press. "Investigation Finds Only 475 Cases of Potential Voter Fraud in Battleground States Won by Biden." *Fortune*, December 14, 2021 (https://fortune.com/2021/12/14/trump-voter-fraud-investigation-biden-battleground-states-only-475-potential-voter-fraud-cases/).

Cathey, Libby. "Trump Suggests Pence Should have 'Overturned' 2020 Election." *ABC News*, January 31, 2022 (https://abcnews.go.com/Politics/trump-suggests-pence-overturned-2020-election/story?id=82581412).

Chavez, Paolo and Benjamin Siegel. "Trump Takes Aim at Sessions for 'Russian Witch Hunt Hoax' in Tweet." *ABC News*, June 5, 2018 (https://abcnews.go.com/Politics/trump-questions-delay-inspector-general-report-rivals-tweet/story?id=55655234).

"Donald Trump Asks Russia to Find Hillary Clinton's Emails," *C-SPAN*, July 27, 2016 (https://www.c-span.org/video/?c4615538/donald-trump-asks-russia-find-hillary-clintons-emails).

"Factbox: Here are Eight Trump Associates Arrested or Convicted of Crimes." *Reuters*, August 20, 2020 (https://www.reuters.com/article/us-usa-trump-bannon-associates-factbox/factbox-here-are-eight-trump-associates-arrested-or-convicted-of-crimes-idUSKBN25G1YU).

Feuer, Alan. "Document in Jan. 6 Case Shows Plan to Storm Government Buildings," *New York Times*, March 14, 2022 (https://www.nytimes.com/2022/03/14/us/politics/enrique-tarrio-jan-6-document.html).

Friedersdorf, Conor. "The Contested Significance of January 6," *The Atlantic*, January 12, 2022 (https://www.theatlantic.com/ideas/archive/2022/01/the-contested-significance-of-january-6/621235).

Holderness, Graham. Nick Potter, and John Turner, *Shakespeare: The Play of History*. Iowa City: University of Iowa Press, 1988.

Kovensky, Josh. "From Nov. 4 to Jan. 6, The MAGA Team Knew Exactly What They Were Doing." *TPM*, April 25, 2022 (https://talkingpointsmemo.com/muckraker/from-nov-4-to-jan-6-the-maga-team-knew-exactly-what-they-were-doing).

Lammers, Lukas. *Shakespearean Temporalities: History on the Early Modern Stage*, Routledge Studies in Shakespeare. New York: Routledge, 2018.

Lowell, Hugo. "Revealed: Trump Reviewed Draft Order that Authorized Voting Machines to be Seized." *The Guardian*, February 4, 2022 (https://www.theguardian.com/us-news/2022/feb/04/trump-draft-order-voting-machines-white-house-meeting).

Luttig, J. Michael. "The Republican Blueprint to Steal the 2024 Election." *CNN*, April 27, 2022 (https://www.cnn.com/2022/04/27/opinions/gop-blueprint-to-steal-the-2024-election-luttig/index.html).

Metz, Sam. "GOP Censures Cheney, Kinzinger as it Assails Jan. 6 probe." *Associated Press*, February 4, 2022 (https://apnews.com/article/donald-trump-salt-lake-city-election-2020-campaign-2016-liz-cheney-cca6eba133e2edee7987cac10e86d5c7).

Pagliery, Jose. "Trump Adviser Peter Navarro Lays Out How He and Bannon Planned to Overturn Biden's Electoral Win." *The Daily Beast*, December 28, 2021 (https://www.thedailybeast.com/trump-advisor-peter-navarro-lays-out-how-he-and-steve-bannon-planned-to-overturn-bidens-electoral-win).

Palmer, Ewan. "Donald Trump Doubles Down on Pardoning Jan. 6 Capitol Rioters, Says Many Not Guilty." *Newsweek*, February 2, 2022 (https://www.newsweek.com/trump-pardon-jan6-capitol-lindsey-graham-newsmax-1675289).

Reilly, Ryan J. "U.S. Wants Prison Time for Rioter Who Said She Would 'Absolutely' Storm Capitol Again." *NBC News*, March 16, 2022 (https://www.nbcnews.com/politics/justice-department/doj-wants-prison-time-rioter-said-absolutely-storm-capitol-rcna19970).

Shakespeare, William. *The Complete Oxford Shakespeare*, edited by Stanley Wells and Gary Taylor. Oxford: Oxford University Press, 1987.

Ulmer, Alexandra and Nathan Layne. "Trump Allies Breach U.S. Voting Systems in Search of 2020 Fraud 'Evidence'." *Reuters*, April 28, 2022 (https://www.reuters.com/investigates/special-report/usa-election-breaches/).

Wheeler, Marcy. "Finally, Everyone Is Talking About Trump's Obstruction on January 6," *Emptywheel*, December 14, 2021 (https://www.emptywheel.net/2021/12/14/finally-everyone-is-talking-about-trumps-obstruction-on-january-6/).

3 The Tyranny of Expectations

Joe Biden has been involved in US politics for a long time. He became a US senator in 1972 at the age of 29 and has been in federal office almost continually since then, with only two short breaks: a brief technical one between the installation of a new Congress and his inauguration as vice-president in 2009, and the four year period between his vice-presidency and presidency. Biden went from being one of the youngest senators ever elected to the oldest president over that fifty-year span, and the US population increased by approximately 125 million, or 60% by US Census estimates.[1] All of which is to say that Joe Biden came to the presidency as a known quantity, with a proven track record and a relatively clear place in the political landscape of the country.

At the same time, Biden's presidency also came with a very clear contrast against the presidency of Donald Trump. Trump was of course president during the only four years out of the past fifty that Biden was not in office. Biden's election as president, then, was both for him and for America likely to be seen as a resumption of past continuity. This in turn brought with it its own expectations for Biden's presidency, both in terms of his own conduct and his political choices.

I do not here wish to suggest that Shakespeare anticipated this particular turn of events, or even anything especially close to it. However, there are multiple Shakespeare plays, centering on two characters, that have a great deal to say about how to manage expectations in a change of governments: the plays leading up to *Henry V* (about Henry V succeeding Henry IV), and *King Lear* (as he prepares to hand the kingdom off to his daughters). As usual, I do not see Biden as directly mirroring any one character in any of these plays. But all these plays collectively show us how Shakespeare approaches this issue, and there are lessons in them for both Biden and us.

DOI: 10.4324/9781003331391-4

The dominant message Shakespeare sends us is this: the contrast with prior expectation is as if not more important to the reception of something new as the actual reality of that new thing. It matters less what Henry V is actually like than how he does or does not live up to people's image of the dissolute Prince Hal, and Hal and the ruling Harry are actually much more alike than they seem. At the same time, Lear shows us that important conversations and negotiations carried out in public can be ruinous, especially when one fails to adapt to disappointed expectations.

Neither of these is surprising, especially in the realm of politics, but they both have significant lessons for the Biden administration. In order to succeed, this would suggest, Biden needs to clearly understand and respond to not just the situation before him but the expectations others bring to his presidency—and in doing so, he must reckon with the difficulties of negotiations that necessarily take place under a certain degree of unwelcome or unhelpful public scrutiny.

From Hal to Harry

The future Henry V is set up across multiple plays as a dissolute young man who no one believes to be actually capable of ruling the country well. This is not a new observation. It is not even a new observation in the context of American politics: George W. Bush had more than his share of comparisons to the transformation Henry Plantagenet undergoes from a brief mention in *Richard II* to the conquest of France in *Henry V*.[2] What I wish to add to this stock observation, then, is an awareness of the way that this apparent transformation overtakes the reality of Henry's kingship, combining our knowledge of the Hal-to-Henry V turn with that strand of scholarship that is deeply skeptical of the value of Henry V's triumphs.

The future Henry V (the version of him I will hereafter call "Hal", as the plays do, to contrast it with the older version of him, "Harry"), first appears in *Richard II*, as a brief reference in the fifth act, serving primarily as a foil to Henry IV's own successes and the more upright character of Henry Percy, son of the Duke of Northumberland. He is described as hanging out with the wrong people and wasting money (5.3.1, 7, 20). But for all that, his father has some hope for his future, though the king cannot and does not actually specify any evidence for this (5.3.21). This sets up the basic Hal dynamic: he is wasting his potential and his youth and creates fears that he will be nothing but a failure as a king, but there is an unreasoned hope that he will somehow make good despite that.

In the two parts of *Henry IV* we see this same character actually appear on stage. We get to meet his companions; we see him party his way through the slums around London, drinking and engaging in pranks that tiptoe over the line into crime; but we also see him tell us (and not his companions) that this is all a show, intended to make him look better in the future (*1 Henry IV* 1.2.198). That is to say, to Hal the friends he makes in lower-class London are temporary. Once he discards them, he believes that the response to his newfound morality will only make him more popular. We see him try this by rejecting his closest friend, Falstaff, in *2 Henry IV* (5.4.47). And it does work, within the limits of the play: the Lord Chief Justice and the other nobles welcome this new Harry as blessedly different from the old Hal, even though audiences often do not agree.[3]

This is a masterpiece of expectations management, even though it has struck generations of critics as troubling.[4] But what I wish to suggest here is that it goes beyond Henry preparing the ground for the transformation between Hal and Harry. There is not nearly as much of a change as the plays and most critics assume. The Harry persona he ends up in is actually not that different from Hal. The work Hal does to prepare for the change, then, not only highlights the contrast between a hypothetical King Hal and the real King Harry but to a certain extent it *creates* that contrast out of whole cloth.

If we focus on Henry V as a ruler (the "Harry" version of him) ignoring, for a moment, his past, we do not necessarily see the good king that he is often made out to be. The first act of *Henry V* is perhaps the clearest evidence of this: Harry is led into declaring war against France by the Archbishop of Canterbury, specifically in order to deflect Harry's attention from the church and the possibility of taxing its wealth (1.1.71–80). The war is comfortably glorious at the end with Harry's near-bloodless (on one side, at least) victory at Agincourt and his total conquest of France. But along the way we see a number of uncomfortable sides of Harry, from his willingness to utterly destroy the town of Harfleur to his personal callousness in not caring that his old friend Bardolph has been hanged for stealing on the march (3.3.91–7, 3.6.108). We also know, as the Chorus helpfully reminds us at the end, that this victory is hollow: the ruinous civil wars that we have already discussed from the *Henry VI* plays come immediately in the wake of Harry's victory.

I suggest that we could read this Harry as a close companion to the dissolute Hal: focused only on his own gain, inattentive to matters of actual governance, and willing to throw away money and manpower on a foreign war that is successful only by the grace of God and the skin of his soldiers' teeth. Had the French not gotten trapped in the mud at Agincourt, or had they refused to fight at all and simply let Harry's sick and starving men die away, Harry would just be "King Hal": a king who does not understand what kingship is, and wastes the blood and treasure of his nation.

There are two reasons we do not typically read Henry V this way. First, he did in fact win, even if the victory was undone within a decade. Second, and more important to the lessons I suggest Shakespeare provides for us, the importance Henry and others place on the Hal-to-Harry transformation obscures the connection between the two parts of his life. Shakespeare's Henry V wants us to see Hal and Harry as two different men, and he works very hard to make them seem so. But the difference between them is often more one of style than of substance.

The last lines of *Henry V* are often surprising to a modern audience because they undercut the triumphs of the rest of the play. While the remainder of the play seems to be, to a large extent, about how awesome Henry V is, this final speech reminds everyone about how impermanent Harry's actual victory was. We will discuss this more in a later chapter; for this one, the key point is that we are reminded not only that "Henry the Sixth ... lost France" (E.9–12), but also that Henry V himself lived only a "small time," which is what led to his son's (or his son's regents') failures (E.5). So while the Chorus urges us to think of Harry as a victor, it cannot help but also remind us that he is a *temporary* victor and that all of the wars he started—and that his death later brought about—"made his England bleed" (E.12). It is an inescapable part of history that Henry V, for all his military greatness, did not really achieve much, especially in the long term.

This should point us, I think, to how much of Henry V's legend is about the expectations of him—how he relates to his own past and to his ancestors'—and how little is about his actual achievements. We are reminded at the start of the play that this sort of military victory has, in fact, been won before under Henry V's great-uncle, the Black Prince (son of Edward III), at Crécy, a battle that was only 69 years before Agincourt (2.4.54–6). This is not to say that it was not a major English victory. But Harry is in the position he is in (not ruling France) despite that earlier victory. And Henry's successors will be in the same spot despite his triumphs, as both we and Shakespeare's audience know. For all the effort he puts into how he is perceived, Henry V's triumph keeps receding out of sight.[5] The narrative of Harry's unique militaristic potency is more propaganda than truth—just like the difference between Harry the king and Hal the prince.

I want to be clear that nothing above is intended to suggest that Henry V's expectation management is wrong in and of itself. The actions involved may be—I would prefer not to defend either hypocritically acquiring friends and casting them off or waging a brutal war of conquest—but the choice to see what people expect of you and react to that is not necessarily wrong. So if there are lessons we can take from Henry's clear-eyed approach to how he will be perceived, I would suggest that they can and should be taken as distinct from the specific actions that he himself takes.

"Nothing can come of nothing"

There is another major Shakespeare play that, as I see it, deals with expectations management, but from the other side: *King Lear*. While Henry V is excellent at manipulating how he will be seen, Lear is awful at it, and also allows his own expectations to blind him to the reality of his daughters' truths and falsehoods. Both in his plans for the future and his execution of the public spectacle of a love test for his daughters, Lear shows us exactly how badly poor expectations management can go. And like Henry V's triumphs, I suggest, the actual difficulties Lear faces are more closely connected to how he makes things seem than how they actually are—at least at the start.

King Lear does not actually begin with the famous scene where Lear asks his daughters to tell him how much they love him. Instead, it starts with a little scene between Kent and Gloucester about the latter's bastard son Edmund. During the course of this short exchange, they let slip that the arrangement Lear is about to pretend is spontaneous in the ensuing scene is in fact highly planned: the "division of the kingdom" (1.1.4) has already been laid out, and Kent and Gloucester, the king's advisors, know about it.[6] The public display of the love test, therefore, is not actually intended as the test it appears to be, but as a choreographed matter of public adulation for the king.

The horrific failure of this supposedly sure thing is therefore our first evidence of how badly Lear mismanages expectations. It is not merely that Cordelia does not give him the answer he wants (though she does not). It is not merely that Lear himself cannot keep his temper in public (though *he* does not). Both of these things are true, and both mean that the public display of affection that Lear has planned for fails. But if that were all, we might think that Lear had simply been blindsided by the results of his love test. This is the tack that Kent takes in trying to reason with Lear (1.1.152).

With the knowledge that this was all pre-planned, however, our eyes are opened up to the full scope of Lear's failure. From any perspective he has exposed himself to unnecessary risk by making the test so public, and his misjudgment of Cordelia's possible answer is also significant, but when we know that he had predetermined the results the magnitude of his error looms even larger. If this idea was really as well-planned as critics have suggested, it seems that a very important player has been left out of that planning.[7] Since he had time to plan all this beforehand and let Kent and Gloucester in on the secret, perhaps he ought to have also tipped off Cordelia? At the very least, while doing so might not have changed her answer (Cordelia seems very sure of her righteousness in limiting her flattery) it might have given him the necessary understanding of her position to correctly parse her statement that she loves him in due proportion to the fact that he "begot me, bred me, loved me" as a declaration of deep love (1.1.96). But he did not do this, and so everything goes awry. The plan itself may be "a sensible and politically astute one," but the fact that it "caught by surprise" one of its major actors (Cordelia) means that its execution was poor.[8] Lear gets ahead of himself, expecting Cordelia to play along with the love test even when he has taken no actual steps to prepare her.

This is typical of Lear. We see it again and again as he winds his way towards madness and death: his expectations of his continued power as king are dashed along with his belief in his other daughters' love and affection (1.4.254–69, 2.2.380–459); his expectations of the larger world melt away on the heath (3.2.14–24, 69–73). These changes in Lear have been noted by many scholars.[9] But what I wish to suggest here is that they are not just changes in his character, but particularly revelations about expectations management. Lear fails because he cannot make others meet his expectations, and does not adjust to that reality quickly enough. He makes things harder on himself by assuming that others will conform to his expectations, most notably his daughters and their husbands. Even when he is reunited with Cordelia, he cannot at first believe it because his expectations of her love have now swung so far in the opposite direction that he thinks she must hate him (5.1.65–8). For Lear, in other words, his expectations and his (mis-)management of them create problems that might have existed on their own (Goneril and Regan would not magically have become kind and generous if he had not expected it) but that he cannot properly deal with because he does not face them head-on.

Senator Joe and President Biden

Biden has had a long career in American politics. He has been accurately described as the most experienced politician to ever take the office of vice-president, and he brought with him into that office an already established political brand.[10] Four years as vice-president did nothing to reduce this familiarity. If anything, it increased it; the satirical magazine *The Onion* featured him throughout his vice-presidency as a kind of everyman, "Diamond Joe" Biden, which may well have contributed to his perceived relatability to voters.[11] Certainly, his decades in the public eye contributed to a sense that Americans knew what they were getting when they elected him: as one biographer put it, for many Biden can be summed up in the simple phrase "'that's Joe,'" which relies entirely on his familiarity.[12]

Unlike Henry V above, those assumptions about Biden tended to be more positive than negative. The "Diamond Joe" stereotype poked fun at Biden and might have downplayed his readiness to actually serve in public office, but it made him seem like an everyday person you could relate to. The more complete political legacy included a hot temper and a brush with plagiarism of campaign speeches, as well as the 1994 crime bill and the ugly Clarence Thomas nomination hearings—but it also included the passage of the Violence Against Women Act and the sheer steadiness of decades in the Senate. The Obama administration in which he served was popular, and Biden's role in it was visible.

It was from this stock, then, that Biden drew when running for president and evidently hoped to draw while serving. His actual campaign promises were quite liberal, but the tone of his campaign was not about those promises. It was all about returning to America before Trump and Covid-19; a "return to normalcy" message like that of Warren Harding exactly a hundred years before.[13] Harding had been referring to both the First World War and the flu pandemic that overlapped it. Biden had his own pandemic to deal with, but he was also banking on his own identity as a key part of that normalcy. It was normal to have Joe Biden running things, and since he'd been part of running them for so long, people could trust that he would bring back normal.

Of course, that normal has not necessarily come back for everyone. The strain of Covid-19 is still being felt. But in political terms, to some extent, Biden has actually met some of those expectations.[14] His handling of political situations has been, well, fairly normal. He's been Joe Biden: unlike Henry V, there have been no claims of massive change from his pre-presidency approach. Perhaps, if we are to take the Hal/Harry continuity seriously, that is a good thing; such claims would be an indication of a *performative* shift, rather than actual evidence that Biden himself had changed. However, since Biden's presidency looks to take advantage of a continuity, rather than a contrast, perhaps we should after all be equally skeptical of the way that he too has managed the expectations with which he was presented.

Public negotiations

Though like Henry V, Biden came into his presidency with pre-existing expectations based on his career, the situation was almost the opposite of Hal's. Biden took office with high approval ratings for the era and correspondingly high expectations. But a confluence of tight margins for error, foreign policy difficulties, and (crucially for this chapter) poor expectations management have led to a reversal in the president's approval ratings. We will address the situation Biden experienced (and continues to experience) in Congress in the next chapter, particularly the equally divided Senate, where Joe Manchin of West Virginia and Kyrsten Sinema of Arizona have carved out their roles as inconstant allies. The foreign policy difficulties surrounding the Afghanistan withdrawal and (to a lesser but still-evolving degree) the Ukraine crisis are the topic of the final chapter. Here I will focus on how Biden has managed and mismanaged public expectations for his presidency. In particular, I wish to look at the degree to which, like Lear, negotiating in public—having a deal you think you have made but that the other party has not actually agreed to yet—has made those expectations both higher and harder to achieve.

Biden has expressed a desire not to "negotiate in the press," but he was not able to avoid doing so to some extent.[15] Unlike Lear, whose very public demand for a love test and equally public description of the lands he would bestow on each daughter was unnecessary since the division had already been made in private, the modern media landscape and particularly the attitudes of both Manchin and Sinema towards the negotiations may have made it impossible for Biden to keep the details of negotiation a secret even if he wanted to. This is doubly true because of the nature of the US Senate, where the filibuster rules meant that an evenly divided Senate could not work through smaller bills for most of Biden's legislative priorities, but had to squeeze them into large comprehensive bills under the process of budget reconciliation, due to concerted Republican intransigence.[16] The reason for that intransigence, of course, is the partisanship discussed in the previous chapters of this book.

So the Democrats, and thus Biden, spent much of the first year of his presidency negotiating in public, if not in the press. Biden held town halls, gave speeches, and answered questions at press conferences; other Democrats also talked to reporters and on talk shows.[17] As we have seen with Lear (though perhaps not to the same degree), this set up a series of expectations about what the Build Back Better Act might include that not only the public but Biden and the rest of the Democratic Party seem to have thought were the true basis of negotiations. Just as Lear seems to think that the conditions he has set and the expectations he has for the future are real—that Cordelia will say she loves him most and his other daughters will allow him a hundred knights and the title of king—so too Biden seemed to believe that simply stating his expectations for the BBB would conjure away the opposition to certain elements of the bill, including its topline scope, from Manchin, Sinema, et al.

This did not work out.

As Lear's experience in the love test shows, negotiating in public is rarely effective, especially when the other party has not agreed to the result of the negotiation in private. As with Lear, I do not wish to suggest here that Biden could have simply achieved his aim by not having the expectations. Manchin and Sinema could very well not have a common ground on which to build any coalition of fifty Senators for the BBB. But Biden did not improve the situation by creating the atmosphere of expectations that public negotiations and public statements of what the BBB would do created, any more than Lear did by his very public love test of Cordelia. Arguably, this also contributed to the much-noted invisibility of other Biden stimulus packages to voters, because all they heard was about the failure of the BBB negotiations, resulting in disappointment.[18] It remains to be seen if the Inflation Reduction Act will resolve this in Biden's favor.

Biden has managed expectations well in terms of his own reputation before the election: a reputation that has seemingly helped him at least weather some of the storms he has encountered. Where he has failed, however, is in this kind of public negotiation, which has led at times to a sense that Biden is not moving the country forward despite his promises.[19] And here, I suggest, we see the lesson of Lear. This is not to say that Biden *is* Lear (Joe Manchin makes an unconvincing Cordelia). But it is a reminder that, like the situation in both *Henry V* and *King Lear*, self-created and self-maintained expectations can only go so far. At some point they come into contact with the beliefs and opinions of those around you, and if you do not plan carefully in private beforehand, a public confrontation has unpredictable and often unpleasant ends. We might, therefore, suggest that Biden should stop relying so much on the pre-existing goodwill that he brought into the office, and instead work carefully, and privately, to enact further legislation. The IRA may be a good start, but the work cannot effectively stop there.

Notes

1 US Bureau of the Census, "Current Population Reports," Series P-25, no. 493. Washington: US Government Printing Office, 1972, https://www.census.gov/content/dam/Census/library/publications/1972/demo/p25-493.pdf, and constantly updating on https://www.census.gov

2 Newstock and Berger, "Harrying," 141–152.

3 James C. Bulman, "*Henry IV, Parts 1* and *2*," in *The Cambridge Companion to Shakespeare's History Plays*, ed. Michael Hattaway (Cambridge: Cambridge University Press, 2002), 174.

4 For a brief overview of the dual nature of Henry/Hal/Harry, and critics' troubled responses to King Harry, see Jelena Mareli, "Revisiting the 'Rabbit-Duck': A Pragma-Rhetorical Approach to Henry's Moral Ambiguity in *Henry V*," *Early Modern Literary Studies* vol. 19, no. 2 (2017): 1–24.

5 Phyllis Rackin, *Stages of History: Shakespeare's English Chronicles* (Ithaca: Cornell University Press, 1990), 29–30.

6 Here I cite the Oxford *Tragedy of King Lear*, based on the Folio, though the analysis would not differ using the Quarto text.

7 Richard Strier, *Resistant Structures: Particularity, Radicalism, and Renaissance Texts* (Berkeley: University of California Press, 1997), 178; Greenblatt, *Tyrant*, 114.

8 Strier, *Resistant Structures*, 178, 180. Strier rightly points out the distinction between the planned division and the love test here: one is reasonable, one a fatal flaw.

9 A good indication of how widespread this observation is might be that Janet Adelman's introduction to *Twentieth Century Interpretations of* King Lear simply takes the changes as a baseline for evaluating the play. Janet Adelman, introduction to *Twentieth Century Interpretations of* King Lear, ed. Janet Adelman (Englewood Cliffs, NJ: Prentice-Hall, Inc., 1978), 5.

10 Jules Witcover, *Joe Biden: A Life of Trial and Redemption* (New York: William Morrow, 2010), 436.

11 Joe Garden, "Area Man Regrets Helping Turn Joe Biden Into a Meme," *Vice*, May 16, 2019 (https://www.vice.com/en/article/xwngb3/area-man-regrets-helping-turn-joe-biden-into-a-meme).

12 Witcover, *Joe Biden*, 484.

13 Ezra Klein, "Joe Biden's promise: a return to normalcy," *Vox*, May 20, 2019 (https://www.vox.com/policy-and-politics/2019/5/20/18631452/joe-biden-2020-presidential-announcement-speech).

14 Jonathan Bernstein, "In Town Hall, Biden Returns to Normalcy," *Bloomberg*, October 22, 2021 (https://www.bloomberg.com/opinion/articles/2021-10-22/in-town-hall-joe-biden-returns-to-normalcy).

15 Sarah Kolinovsky, "Biden pulls back curtain on spending negotiations with Democrats," *ABC News*, October 22, 2021 (http://abcnews.go.com/Politics/biden-pulls-back-curtain-spending-negotiations-democrats/story?id=80727626).

16 Michael Tomasky, "Can He Build Back Better," *New York Review of Books,* February 10, 2022 (http://www.nybooks.com/articles/2022/02/10/can-he-build-back-better).
17 See Kolinovsky; Tomasky; Ed Pilkington, "Democrats brace for bruising October talks as Biden agenda stalls in Congress," *The Guardian*, October 3, 2021 (https://www.theguardian.com/us-news/2021/oct/03/democrats-negotat ions-october-biden-agenda-stalls-congress).
18 Alexander Burns, "If Biden's Plan Is Like a 'New Deal,' Why Don't Voters Care?", *New York Times*, April 21, 2022 (http://www.nytimes.com/2022/04/21/us/politics/biden-pandemic-relief-democrats.html); David Smith, "'We need him to deliver': Biden faces wrath of disappointed supporters," *The Guardian*, October 23, 2021 (https://www.theguardian.com/us-news/2021/oct/23/joe-biden-disappointed-supporters-approval).
19 Bill de Blasio, "Joe Biden Can Learn From My Mistakes," *The Atlantic*, May 3, 2022 (https://www.theatlantic.com/ideas/archive/2022/05/bill-de-blasio-joe-biden-approval-2022-midterms/629740/).

References

Adelman, Janet. *Introduction to Twentieth Century Interpretations of* King Lear. Edited by Janet Adelman, pp. 1–21. Englewood Cliffs, NJ: Prentice-Hall, Inc., 1978.

Bernstein, Jonathan. "In Town Hall, Biden Returns to Normalcy." *Bloomberg*, October 22, 2021 (https://www.bloomberg.com/opinion/articles/2021-10-22/in-town-hall-joe-biden-returns-to-normalcy).

de Blasio, Bill. "Joe Biden Can Learn From My Mistakes." *The Atlantic*, May 3, 2022 (https://www.theatlantic.com/ideas/archive/2022/05/bill-de-blasio-joe-biden-approval-2022-midterms/629740/).

Bulman, James C. "*Henry IV, Parts 1* and *2.*" In *The Cambridge Companion to Shakespeare's History Plays*, edited by Michael Hattaway, pp. 158–176. Cambridge: Cambridge University Press, 2002.

Burns, Alexander. "If Biden's Plan Is Like a 'New Deal,' Why Don't Voters Care?" *New York Times*, April 21, 2022 (http://www.nytimes.com/2022/04/21/us/politics/biden-pandemic-relief-democrats.html).

Garden, Joe. "Area Man Regrets Helping Turn Joe Biden Into a Meme." *Vice*, May 16, 2019 (https://www.vice.com/en/article/xwngb3/area-man-regrets-helping-turn-joe-biden-into-a-meme).

Greenblatt, Stephen. *Tyrant: Shakespeare on Politics.* New York: WW Norton, 2018.

Klein, Ezra. "Joe Biden's Promise: A Return to Normalcy." *Vox*, May 20, 2019 (https://www.vox.com/policy-and-politics/2019/5/20/18631452/joe-biden-2020-presidential-announcement-speech).

Kolinovsky, Sarah. "Biden Pulls Back Curtain on Spending Negotiations with Democrats." *ABC News*, October 22, 2021 (http://abcnews.go.com/Politics/biden-pulls-back-curtain-spending-negotiations-democrats/story?id=80727626).

Marelj, Jelena. "Revisiting the 'Rabbit-Duck': A Pragma-Rhetorical Approach to Henry's Moral Ambiguity in *Henry V*." *Early Modern Literary Studies* 19, no. 2 (2017): 1–24.

Newstok, Scott L. and Harry Berger, Jr., "Harrying After VV," In *Shakespeare After 9/11: How a Social Trauma Reshapes Interpretation, Shakespeare Yearbook* 20, edited by Douglas A. Brooks, Matthew Biberman, and Julia Reinhard Lupton, pp. 141–152. Lewiston: Edwin Mellen, 2011.

Pilkington, Ed. "Democrats brace for bruising October talks as Biden agenda stalls in Congress." *The Guardian*, October 3, 2021 (https://www.theguardian.com/us-news/2021/oct/03/democrats-negotations-october-biden-agenda-stalls-congress).

Rackin, Phyllis. *Stages of History: Shakespeare's English Chronicles*. Ithaca: Cornell University Press, 1990.

Shakespeare, William. *The Complete Oxford Shakespeare*, edited by Stanley Wells and Gary Taylor. Oxford: Oxford University Press, 1987.

Smith, David. "'We Need Him to Deliver': Biden Faces Wrath of Disappointed Supporters." *The Guardian*, October 23, 2021 (https://www.theguardian.com/us-news/2021/oct/23/joe-biden-disappointed-supporters-approval).

Strier, Richard. *Resistant Structures: Particularity, Radicalism, and Renaissance Texts*. Berkeley: University of California Press, 1997.

Tomasky, Michael. "Can He Build Back Better." *New York Review of Books*, February 10, 2022 (http://www.nybooks.com/articles/2022/02/10/can-he-build-back-better).

US Bureau of the Census, "Current Population Reports," Series P-25, no. 493. Washington: US Government Printing Office, 1972. https://www.census.gov/content/dam/Census/library/publications/1972/demo/p25-493.pdf

Witcover, Jules. *Joe Biden: A Life of Trial and Redemption*. New York: William Morrow, 2010.

4 Inconstant Coalitions

The public negotiations in the last chapter are, of course, entirely internal to the Democratic party; the Republicans have opposed much of the Biden agenda in lockstep. This kind of need for internal coalition-building is actually normal party behavior in the modern era, but it is particularly significant given the peculiar situation in Washington. As a result of the November 2020 elections and the January 2021 runoffs in Georgia, the Democrats control not only the White House but a slim majority in the House of Representatives and an even fifty-fifty split in the Senate broken by Vice President Kamala Harris. They, therefore, hold the so-called "trifecta" that allows a party in power to pass bills through both houses of Congress and have them signed by the President into law. And they have used this power. But given the arcane rules of the US Senate, which in regular order requires a supermajority of 60 votes to end debate, and the narrowness of both majorities, which allows small groups of potential defectors to wield great leverage, Biden's presidency so far has been less a glorious use of the trifecta to enact his entire agenda and more a series of protracted, often public, negotiations around the exacting details of large bills intended to be passed through budget reconciliation, a parliamentary tactic that gets around the filibuster, and about negotiations around the filibuster itself. As such, there have been repeated references in the political press to Biden's presidency as being dominated not by Biden but by the two most recalcitrant Democratic senators, Sinema and especially Manchin.[1]

Shakespeare rarely, if ever, shows us the sausage-making that goes into representative government. Part of this is because his own England had not fully developed the modern parliamentary system into which its model of the king-in-Parliament would eventually evolve; parliaments were not held every year, and England was at most a middle ground between absolute monarchy and a real republic. We can see this in the words of the famous early Renaissance legal scholar John Fortescue, for

DOI: 10.4324/9781003331391-5

whom England was a "politic and regall" nation, poised between "regal" absolute France and "politic" republican Venice.[2] This cannot be the whole reason, of course. Shakespeare's plays are not actually set in his own England, and his contemporary Ben Jonson showed exactly this kind of political wrangling in the Roman senate in both *Sejanus* and *Catiline*, set in much the same Rome in which Shakespeare set his own Roman plays. But whatever the reason, Shakespeare's depictions of republican representative lawmaking are limited to a few moments in the third scene of *Othello* (1.3.1–46).[3]

But while Shakespeare does not show us any exact parallels for Biden's dealmaking with Sinema, Manchin, and the rest of Congress, by this point in the book I hope I have convinced you that we should be well past needing to look for such exactitude. And what Shakespeare omits in dealing with the process of legislation, he provides in a form much more familiar to his contemporary English audiences: the coalition building among noble houses in the War of the Roses. Shakespeare shows us coalition-building elsewhere, notably in *Julius Caesar*—Cassius woos Brutus quite effectively—but not to quite the same extent. And while, as we have already seen, bringing Brutus onto his side leads Cassius's cause astray because of Brutus's out-of-date political instincts, the histories show a different side of the situation. There, the difficulties come less because of any one character's political missteps after the alliances are made than because of the way in which they break. These plays thereby provide dramatic lessons for the potentially frayed alliances of contemporary government even as they depict the imagined reality of medieval England, not modern America.

In particular, I suggest that the use of three major characters across the War of the Roses cycle should have specific resonance with contemporary politics. The rise and fall of Warwick, Clarence, and Buckingham in *2 & 3 Henry VI* and *Richard III* should warn us about the dangers of misaligned and mismanaged coalitions. But so too should the fates of the kings they serve, from Henry VI and Edward IV to Richard III himself. None of these characters leave their plays alive, and while the personal stakes may not be quite that high for Biden and the senators, we can all hope that the lessons Shakespeare provides by showing faulty coalition-building in his plays might lead to a more satisfactory ending if applied correctly.

Powerful allies

One of the most significant non-royal characters in Shakespeare's history plays is Richard Neville, Earl of Warwick: Warwick the Kingmaker, as he has come to be known. In the *Henry VI* plays, Warwick stands between the two competing houses of Lancaster and York that are vying for the crown, and both sides believe that his power, combined with their own, will be enough to overcome their enemies. In this section, I will briefly look at how Shakespeare depicts Warwick's power and his shifting alliances—along with the similar shifts of two other characters, the Dukes of Clarence and Buckingham—and examine what we might take from these negotiations about the nature of political alliances more broadly.

Warwick is an early adopter of Richard of York's cause. He is present in the fateful scene in the rose garden that we looked at earlier, where he and his father swear allegiance to York (*2 Henry VI*, 2.2.60–1). He and York exchange promises to support and raise one another (2.2.79, 81–2). When the War of the Roses comes to actual armed combat, Warwick takes the field with York, and it is he (and not York) who gets the celebratory speech at the end of *2 Henry VI*, declaring their victory at St. Albans (5.5.33–38), as well as the first words of *3 Henry VI* (1.1.1). Early in the latter play he repeats his intent to king York, and it is by his encouragement that York sits down on Henry VI's throne (1.1.48–9). It is Warwick, more than York, whose power allows for that audacity: as Henry VI says, York only acts "backed by the power of Warwick" (1.1.52). In the ensuing debate over the right to the crown, it is Warwick whose voice is strongest on York's side. And it is Warwick's troops who flood the throne room and force Henry to name York his heir (1.1.167–70).

Even with York's death in the ensuing fighting, Warwick holds his place in the alliance. It is he, not York's heir, the future Edward IV, who knows the details of how the Yorkist cause is doing (2.1.104–200). He and Edward renew the vows of mutual support that had existed between him and Richard of York, in greater detail (2.3.29–41). And as part of that support, Warwick proposes to negotiate an alliance for Edward with France through marriage (2.6.89–98). Edward agrees, telling him he will consult with him on all future decisions (2.6.101–2). But this agreement does not last long.

In the second scene after Warwick's departure for France, Edward meets Lady Gray, falls in love, or at least lust, and promises to marry her. In the next scene, Warwick negotiates for the hand of Lady Bona and the alliance with France—only to find out by letters that Edward has already married Lady Gray. And the alliance that had seemed so strong is over. As Helen Patricia Maskew has noted, Shakespeare compresses this from a historically slow, eight-year disaffection of Warwick from Edward to a near-instant turn upon receipt of the letters.[4] Warwick declares Edward "no more my king, for he dishonours me" (3.3.184). He raises the French troops he had come to ask for to help Edward, but now to fight against him.

But Warwick is not the only one who abandons Edward for this betrayal. George, Duke of Clarence and Edward's brother, defects too. Perhaps it would be more accurate to say that Edward pushes Clarence away, insisting that as king he must have his way (4.1.15–6). By doing this in this manner, he loses allies: Warwick, Henry VI, and Clarence quickly unite through marriage (Warwick's two daughters to Henry's son and Clarence), and the balance of power shifts away from Edward. Warwick and Clarence quickly rally others to Henry's banner.

They do so in Henry's name, but it is clearly Warwick who is in command here: the troops cry out his name more than Henry's (4.2.27–9, 4.3.26 s.d.) and it is he, not Henry, who gets to vent his anger at the captured Edward (4.4.4–13, 21–30). When Edward escapes, it is his and Clarence's allies who they count on, not Henry's (4.9.9–16). And in 5.1, it is Warwick who banters with Edward and his brother, the future Richard III, about the relative strengths of their claims and their armies. Henry is a figurehead; Warwick's change of parties is what matters, not some sudden resurgence in Henry's power.

But while Warwick has enough power to turn the tide of the war, he overplays his hand by his own excessive reliance on an ally: in this case, Clarence. Clarence turns back to his brother, abandoning Warwick and Henry when they need him. Clarence may have married into Warwick's family and sworn allegiance to him (5.1.92). But he goes back to his brothers, ironically while declaring "I will henceforth be no more unconstant" (5.1.105). The triple-cross functionally ends the war, as Warwick dies in the next scene, followed quickly by Henry's son and then Henry himself.

Yet all is not well for Clarence, either. He ends *3 Henry VI* in his brother's favor for having turned the war but begins *Richard III* being taken to the Tower, because of Edward's paranoia and his brother Richard's machinations. There Richard arranges for him to be killed under Edward's orders (1.4.88–94). The murderers speak to him of his "false forswearing," though it is unclear whether they mean to Edward, Henry, or Warwick (1.4.197). And ultimately he ends up drowned in a butt of malmsey wine. Only two scenes later, Edward dies of illness, clearing the main cast of the Warwick-York story off the stage.

Just as Clarence is dying in the Tower and Edward in his palace, we are introduced to another character whose political support is vital to a king, and who will end up dying for a revolt against him. This time the king is not Edward IV but his brother and successor, Richard III, and his ally is the Duke of Buckingham. Buckingham is Richard's closest and first supporter, and the breaking of their alliance leads, ultimately, to both their deaths.

Buckingham is, initially, an astute political partner of Richard's, and his help is invaluable first in eliminating the other power players, most notably Hastings, and then in actually putting Richard on the throne. It is Buckingham who spreads the lies that are used to justify placing Richard on the throne, and Buckingham who brings the local leaders of London in to proclaim Richard's right (3.5.70–95, 3.7.1–55). Shakespeare particularly focuses on the degree to which they work together to bring Richard's plans to fruition.[5] The play has no depiction of Parliament, let alone the US houses of Congress, but we might well think of Buckingham as fulfilling the role of a good legislative ally to Richard's executive in the American model where the executive branch cannot directly create law itself (the ever-encroaching mass of executive orders aside). Richard has ideas about how England should be ruled, but it is Buckingham who largely makes it possible for him to execute them.

Until, that is, Buckingham reaches his stopping point: Richard's desire to have the princes in the Tower killed. In this moment of Buckingham and Richard falling out, we learn a great deal about how they *used to* work together. Buckingham has been acting under the promise of reward—the Earldom of Hereford—in exchange for enacting Richard's will. But he has not yet received it, and during the tense exchange between them over the princes, Richard reneges on the deal (4.3.86–121). Buckingham responds by announcing his plan to leave Richard.

Of course, he does more than leave Richard: he rebels. Buckingham raises troops in Wales (4.3.47–8) to support the invading army of the future Henry VII. But his army is destroyed offstage and without any difficulty (4.4.442–4). Buckingham had power operating in concert with Richard, but he vastly overestimated that power when he broke from him.

But then again, perhaps Richard also overestimated his power without Buckingham. For all that Richard's power is sufficient to wipe Buckingham out, the lack of Buckingham by his side is arguably also crucial to Richard's own defeat. Without Buckingham, Richard is functionally isolated: he has minions to do his bidding, but no true allies with whom to plan. His isolation is emphasized by the succession of spirits who appear to him the night before Bosworth Field. Buckingham is the culmination of these (Clarence also makes an appearance), and it is on his words that Richard wakes to the despair that all the ghosts have wished on him (5.5.121–6). Richard's inability to give Buckingham what he promised is cast for us as his last and most crucial betrayal. The other spirits speak only of his cruelty; Buckingham reminds us and Richard that he "helped [him] to the crown" (5.5.121). Without that help—without Buckingham's support—Richard falls at Bosworth as his nobles abandon him.

Wavering commitments

Buckingham and the other nobles may have abandoned Richard; the same cannot be said of Biden and his key senators. He has had the support of both Manchin and Sinema for many votes. First and foremost, they support Chuck Schumer as Senate Majority Leader, meaning that Mitch McConnell, the "Grim Reaper" of legislation is not setting the Senate schedule.[6] But both Manchin and Sinema have supported Biden's COVID stimulus, the American Rescue Plan; the Bipartisan Infrastructure Framework; a whole litany of judges, including most recently the confirmation of Ketanji Brown Jackson to the Supreme Court; and most, though not all, of Biden's executive branch nominations as well.

But when it has come to the broader strokes of Biden's agenda, encapsulated most obviously in the Build Back Better Act, both Manchin and Sinema have balked. In addition to opposing filibuster reform, which would reduce the stakes of any one particular bill, they have taken turns opposing elements of the proposal, cutting it down in size (though they did eventually pass part of it as the Inflation Reduction Act). Manchin in particular has been vocal in his opposition to the remaining parts of the proposal, while Sinema has been less forthcoming in the details of what she might oppose.[7] In addition, Manchin, though not Sinema, opposed the Women's Health Protection Act that would have codified abortion rights nationally.[8] And as a result, while they have been invaluable bulwarks against united Republican obstruction in some areas, they have also appeared to ally themselves with those Republicans against the Biden administration in others. This gives the impression of a wavering commitment to the Biden agenda, especially under the conditions of intense partisanship described above.

Obviously, these conditions are not the same as those of the War of the Roses. Opposing the BBB and thus sinking Biden's approval numbers is not equivalent to Warwick, Clarence, or Buckingham literally leading armies into the field to attempt to defeat and kill their former king. But at the same time, either Manchin or Sinema changing parties (a possibility that Republicans have floated, though neither senator has as yet taken the bait) would be just as devastating, though in a different context, as Warwick's, Clarence's, or Buckingham's switches of allegiance. The ability to set the legislative agenda is important, even if it does not guarantee passing that agenda, as are committee chairships and all the other perks that come with being the Senate majority—not to mention the benefit of incumbency when an election rolls around, as it inevitably does. There is therefore much to be gained for the Biden administration and the Democratic party from looking at how to keep recalcitrant members in the fold—and, conversely, for Manchin and Sinema to see what happens to all involved when those allegiances snap.

My 80% friend

Former President Ronald Reagan is believed to have said that "someone who agrees with me 80% of the time is my 80% friend, not my 20% enemy."[9] This is usually quoted (as it is in my source for the quote) as an admonishment towards contemporary politicians, or sometimes primary voters, who are accused of mistaking who their true enemies are. Its application is fairly straightforward: politicians like Manchin and Sinema, who vote with their party most of the time but not all of it, are still a benefit to the party because they can move large parts of its agenda forward despite blocking some portions of it. Judges, the American Rescue Plan, the Bipartisan Infrastructure Framework the IRA, and control of the Senate agenda play the role of the 80% here; the rest of the BBB, the filibuster, certain regulatory nominations, and the WHPA (for Manchin at least) play the role of the 20%. Of course, logically it could go the other way too: not only does it suggest Biden should tolerate Manchin's and Sinema's occasional defections but also that they in turn should accept the times that Biden publicly disagrees with them.

One thing we might notice after paying careful attention to the Shakespeare plays above, however, is that this saying misses out on which elements of agreement or disagreement matter to whom. Warwick and Edward IV are 80% allies, but the other 20% includes Edward making a fool of Warwick's embassy to France (from Warwick's perspective). Edward thinks that they are still allies, that he can paper over the disagreement and still marry the woman he chooses rather than the one Warwick was strategically negotiating a marriage alliance to. Warwick, however, thinks that Edward has crossed a line, regardless of the degree of their remaining agreement. This line comes at his embassy being undercut, not at any of the war or violence that he has willingly participated in. Similarly, though perhaps to less sympathy from the audience, Buckingham remains committed to Richard III's reign despite the order to kill the princes (he denies and delays, but he is not planning rebellion) and his key 20% comes in the form of the earldom of Hereford. These incidents suggest that here it is not, as Reagan asserted, the overall percentage of agreement that matters politically, but what you agree and disagree about, and how important each part is to each player.

We might consider in this connection whether the particular items that Manchin and Sinema have stood out against are sufficiently central to Biden's agenda—or, conversely, whether Biden's responses (such as naming and shaming Manchin's involvement in the defeat of the bill) are sufficiently important to Manchin and/or Sinema—to justify turning from ally to enemy. It is unlikely that Manchin will respond to being blamed by Biden for the BBB's failure by raising a West Virginian army against Biden's presidency, of course, in the mode of Warwick and Edward, but the possibility of a party switch has been raised not just by pundits but by other senators.[10] There is historical precedent for such a switch in the form of Arlen Specter and especially Jim Jeffords, who changed parties in 2009 and 2001 respectively, with Jeffords' switch giving Democrats control of the chamber instead of Republicans.[11] For the record, Manchin's response has been to call this possibility "bull—", though he has floated the possibility of becoming independent while remaining caucused with the Democrats.[12]

Regardless of what Manchin decides (or whether Sinema does anything similar), the question remains: where is the breaking point? An 80% ally is not necessarily an ally if the 80% is less important than the rest; sheer volume does not dictate political decisions alone. On the one hand, as David Karol has argued, political parties are often made up of smaller groups with strongly held positions on individual issues.[13] On the other, as Shakespeare's plays attest, is it is sometimes issues like honor and respect, not overlapping interests, that will direct changes in alliances. Indeed, these are often the less predictable kinds of partisan realignments.[14] Manchin going onto Fox News to discuss his "no" vote on the Build Back Better Act, and the Biden administration's choice to publicly air some of the few non-public elements of their negotiations in response, show that these issues have not aged out of our politics since Shakespeare.[15]

The language used to make a criticism; the timing of a break from an ally; the details of exactly who said what to whom and when; these are all more important than we often like to pretend they are. A narrow coalition like the one Biden leads is inherently difficult to maintain. Of course, so is the position of a senator like Manchin who serves a state his party's presidential candidate lost by double digits. One thing Shakespeare shows us consistently, however, is that turning on each other is not likely to improve either party's situation: Warwick, Clarence, the two Richards of York, Edward, and Buckingham all falter more alone than they do together. Likewise, we might see that turning back and forth—the inconstancy that Clarence accuses himself of—does not work well either: after a very public break, coming together again does not necessarily heal all wounds with your allies or with the public. And indeed, after the failure of the BBB the Democrats initially looked poised to lose heavily in November 2022, regardless of the IRA resuscitating a portion of it.

Therefore, we might suggest that it would be valuable for them to look to find further common ground now, if it is still there to find. Perhaps Warwick and Edward could not have worked together any longer, but by actively fighting, they only made things worse for England, and for each other—just as, remembering *Julius Caesar*, Cassius's and Brutus's arguments weaken their side as well. A similar lesson here would suggest that Manchin, Sinema, and Biden might not be able to reverse their political woes by working together, but that they have little chance of any success if they continue to work separately. Shakespeare's kings and their supporters sometimes fail despite maintaining their alliances, but their odds are far worse when their coalitions fall apart.

Notes

1 See the examples cited in John T. Bennett, "Why it's time to retire the 'Joe Manchin is the real president' narrative," *Roll Call*, December 21, 2021 (https://rollcall.com/2021/12/21/why-its-time-to-retire-the-joe-manchin-is-the-real-president-narrative/).

2 John Fortescue, *A learned commendation of the politique lawes of Englande,* translated by Robert Mulcaster (London: Richard Tottill, 1567), 83v.

3 For more on the Venetian republic in that scene, see Philip C. McGuire, '*Othello* as an "Assay of Reason"', *Shakespeare Quarterly* 24, no. 2 (1973), 199–200; Mark Matheson, 'Venetian Culture and the Politics of *Othello*', *Shakespeare Survey* 48 (1995): 128.

4 Helen Patricia Maskew, "Shakespeare and the Earl of Warwick: The Kingmaker in the *Henry VI* Trilogy" (Ph. D. Dissertation, University of Birmingham, 2009), 202–4, 234–8.

5 Walsh, *Queen's Men,* 152; Greenblatt, *Tyrant,* 76–8.

6 Camilo Montoya-Galvez, "'Think of me as the Grim Reaper': McConnell vows to thwart Democratic proposals," *CBS News*, April 22, 2019 (https://www.cbsnews.com/news/mitch-mcconnell-vows-to-be-the-grim-reaper-to-thwart-all-democratic-proposals/).

7 Tomasky, "Can He."
8 Deepa Shivaram, "A bill to codify abortion protections fails in the Senate," *NPR*, May 11, 2022 (https://www.npr.org/2022/05/11/1097980529/senate-to-vote-on-a-bill-that-codifies-abortion-protections-but-it-will-likely-f).
9 Morris P. Fiorina with Samuel J. Abrams, *Disconnect: The Breakdown of Representation in American Politics* (Norman: University of Oklahoma Press, 2009), 38.
10 Dave Goldiner, "GOP Woos Sen. Joe Manchin to switch parties after blow up over Biden spending plan," *New York Daily News*, December 22, 2021 (https://www.nydailynews.com/news/politics/us-elections-government/ny-joe-manchin-mitch-mcconnell-republican-senate-democratic-biden-20211222-evwgiwtwqjf7viezkkug7erml4-story.html).
11 Daniel Nasaw, "Pennsylvania senator Arlen Specter switches party to become Democrat," *The Guardian*, April 28, 2009 (https://www.theguardian.com/world/2009/apr/28/arlen-specter-republican-democrat-senate); Paul Kane, "How Jim Jeffords single-handedly bent the arc of politics," *Washington Post*, August 18, 2014 (https://www.washingtonpost.com/news/the-fix/wp/2014/08/18/how-jim-jeffords-single-handedly-bent-the-arc-of-politics/).
12 Alexander Bolton, "Manchin on party switch: 'It's bull—," *The Hill*, October 20, 2021 (https://thehill.com/homenews/senate/577623-manchin-on-party-switch-its-bull/); Barbara Sprunt, "Manchin says he offered to change political parties if he was a 'problem' for Dems," *NPR*, October 21, 2021 (https://www.npr.org/2021/10/21/1048121435/manchin-says-he-offered-to-change-political-parties-if-he-was-a-problem-for-dems).
13 David Karol, *Party Position Change in American Politics: Coalition Management* (Cambridge: Cambridge University Press, 2009), 183.
14 Karol, *Party*, 8.
15 Teaganne Finn and Julie Tsurkin, "Manchin says he's a 'no' on Biden's Build Back Better legislation, puncturing hopes for its passage," *NBC News*, December 19, 2021 (https://www.nbcnews.com/politics/congress/manchin-says-he-no-biden-s-build-back-better-legislation-n1286281).

References

Bennett, John T. "Why It's Time to Retire the 'Joe Manchin is the Real President' Narrative." *Roll Call*, December 21, 2021 (https://rollcall.com/2021/12/21/why-its-time-to-retire-the-joe-manchin-is-the-real-president-narrative/).

Bolton, Alexander. "Manchin on Party Switch: 'It's Bull—." *The Hill*, October 20, 2021 (https://thehill.com/homenews/senate/577623-manchin-on-party-switch-its-bull/).

Finn, Teaganne and Julie Tsurkin. "Manchin Says He's a 'No' on Biden's Build Back Better Legislation, Puncturing Hopes for its Passage." *NBC News*, December 19, 2021 (https://www.nbcnews.com/politics/congress/manchin-says-he-no-biden-s-build-back-better-legislation-n1286281).

Fiorina, Morris P. with Samuel J. Abrams. *Disconnect: The Breakdown of Representation in American Politics.* Norman: University of Oklahoma Press, 2009.

Fortescue, John. *A Learned Commendation of the Politique Lawes of Englande*, translated by Robert Mulcaster. London, 1567.

Goldiner, Dave. "GOP Woos Sen. Joe Manchin to Switch Parties After Blow Up Over Biden Spending Plan." *New York Daily News*, December 22, 2021 (https://www.nydailynews.com/news/politics/us-elections-government/ny-joe-manchin-mitch-mcconnell-republican-senate-democratic-biden-20211222-evwgiwtwqjf7viezkkug7erml4-story.html).

Greenblatt, Stephen. *Tyrant: Shakespeare on Politics*. New York: WW Norton, 2018.

Karol, David. *Party Position Change in American Politics: Coalition Management*. Cambridge: Cambridge University Press, 2009.

Maskew, Helen Patricia. "Shakespeare and the Earl of Warwick: The Kingmaker in the *Henry VI* Trilogy." Ph. D. Dissertation, University of Birmingham, 2009.

Matheson, Mark. 'Venetian Culture and the Politics of *Othello*', *Shakespeare Survey* 48 (1995): 123–133.

McGuire, Philip C. '*Othello* as an "Assay of Reason"', *Shakespeare Quarterly* 24, no. 2 (1973): 198–209.

Montoya-Galvez, Camilo. "'Think of Me as the Grim Reaper': McConnell Vows to Thwart Democratic Proposals." *CBS News*, April 22, 2019 (https://www.cbsnews.com/news/mitch-mcconnell-vows-to-be-the-grim-reaper-to-thwart-all-democratic-proposals/).

Nasaw, Daniel. "Pennsylvania Senator Arlen Specter Switches Party to Become Democrat." *The Guardian*, April 28, 2009 (https://www.theguardian.com/world/2009/apr/28/arlen-specter-republican-democrat-senate).

Shakespeare, William. *The Complete Oxford Shakespeare*, edited by Stanley Wells and Gary Taylor. Oxford: Oxford University Press, 1987.

Shivaram, Deepa. "A Bill to Codify Abortion Protections Fails in the Senate." *NPR*, May 11, 2022 (https://www.npr.org/2022/05/11/1097980529/senate-to-vote-on-a-bill-that-codifies-abortion-protections-but-it-will-likely-f).

Sprunt, Barbara. "Manchin Says He Offered to Change Political Parties If He was a 'Problem' for Dems." *NPR*, October 21, 2021 (https://www.npr.org/2021/10/21/1048121435/manchin-says-he-offered-to-change-political-parties-if-he-was-a-problem-for-dems).

Tomasky, Michael. "Can He Build Back Better." *New York Review of Books*, February 10, 2022 (http://www.nybooks.com/articles/2022/02/10/can-he-build-back-better).

Walsh, Brian. *Shakespeare, the Queen's Men, and the Elizabethan Performance of History*. Cambridge: Cambridge University Press, 2009.

5 Illegitimate Justice

One of the most significant difficulties for the Biden presidency has been the federal judiciary system, which has been stacked with Republican appointees over the years by the vagaries of the nominating process.[1] This has already led to multiple cases, particularly out of the Fifth Circuit Court of Appeals, where the efforts of the Biden administration and Democratic policymakers and interest groups in diverse areas such as abortion, immigration, and pandemic responses have been stymied by an actively oppositional judiciary.[2]

This has been particularly significant because of the composition of the final court of appeal in the US judicial system, the Supreme Court. Donald Trump appointed three of the nine justices to the court. One of these, Neil Gorsuch, was appointed to a seat held open by a Republican Senate which refused to even hold hearings for the appointment of Merrick Garland by Barack Obama.[3] The principle cited was that voters should be allowed to weigh in on the appointment of a Supreme Court Justice during a presidential election year.[4] Another, Amy Coney Barrett, was appointed, confirmed, and seated within a month, during an election year, with her confirmation coming a bare two weeks before Trump lost the 2020 presidential election.[5] Evidently the same principle no longer applied.

Unsurprisingly, William Shakespeare has nothing to say to us about the make-up of the Supreme Court. But he has rather a lot to say about stacking the deck in a court of law and making sure a case is decided in the way you want while claiming to be doing nothing of the sort. And what Shakespeare's examples give us is the potentially depressing conclusion that this usually goes very well for the parties who take advantage of the court. If Biden and the Democratic party, therefore, wish to overcome the judicial roadblock of a stacked Supreme Court, Shakespeare's plays would suggest that the answer is in making the court over in their preferred image—by court-stacking, impeachments,

DOI: 10.4324/9781003331391-6

or whatever other techniques might be imagined—rather than in clinging to the assumption that a good legal argument will win the day.

The Queen and the Jew

At first glance, Katharine of Aragon and Shylock of Venice have relatively little in common: a Spanish princess married off to Henry VIII and then shockingly divorced on the one hand; a Jewish moneylender in Italy who loses first his daughter and then his fortune and religion on the other. But they have one massive similarity in Shakespeare: both of them are on the losing end of major legal decisions. In both cases, the audience's sensibility—at least our modern one—is on that losing side. And in both cases, the court proceeds to judgment despite obvious judicial bias.

In both cases, the judge of the case has a direct interest in its outcome. Katharine is first faced with Cardinal Wolsey as her judge, a man she calls her "most malicious foe"; no wonder then, that she twice demands to his face that he not be the judge of her case (2.4.81, 80, 116). After Wolsey's fall—ironically because he tried to slow the decision against her (3.2.30–6)—she is judged offstage by men handpicked by her husband, Henry VIII, making the system even less impartial since he is a party to the case (4.1.24–33). Shylock has no such opportunity to know the identity of his judge; he believes he is being judged by a young doctor of laws called Balthasar, when in fact he is being judged by the wife of one of the people opposed to him (4.1.149–165). Portia, Bassanio's wife, has disguised herself as a judge and come to pass a particularly strained form of justice against the man who threatens her husband's best friend.

It would seem in both cases that recusal would be the only appropriate solution, but Henry VIII and Wolsey reject it and Portia never considers it. For Wolsey, the answer to Katharine's righteous anger is for her to calm herself (a misogynist trope itself, that the angry woman is the problem and not the cause of her anger) (2.4.99–100). Henry, far from distancing himself, is the central character in procuring his own divorce. Portia, of course, not only fails to recuse but actively pursues the opportunity to abuse justice in this case.

And yet, though these cases can hardly pretend to produce true *justice*, both Shylock and Katharine receive *judgment* at these biased hands, and the endings of the plays treat those judgments positively. Henry VIII gets divorced from Katharine, and the play ends with a prophetic vision of the triumphant future awaiting the child born by the woman he marries after the divorce: Elizabeth I, daughter of Anne Boleyn (5.4.14–62). Portia quibbles over blood and flesh and finds a law that somehow frees Antonio of all obligation while forcing Shylock to lose his money and convert to Christianity in exchange for his life (4.1.321–9, 343–60). She goes home to Belmont in the next act to chide her husband for not recognizing her, but the play ends on what seems to want to be a happy note with the passing of Shylock's fortune to his converted daughter Jessica and her husband Lorenzo.

Both of these endings have received criticism over the years. In *Henry VIII*, Katharine consistently comes across as a sympathetic character, and her treatment as unjust.[6] Likewise, there is a whole cottage industry of legal and literary scholars debating the injustice of Shylock's situation.[7] So to the audience, these happy endings do not seem as happy as the plays want them to be. But for all the ambiguity that these audience reactions might produce in us, it is inarguable, I think, that within the worlds of the plays these unjust legal victories are fairly complete: no one on stage is left arguing for Katharine or condemning Shylock's treatment.

I suggest, in fact, that this points us in the direction of what Richard Strier has called Shakespeare's discomfort with legal systems.[8] These legal systems *judge*, but they do not provide *justice*. And I agree with Strier that this is Shakespeare's great insight into legal systems as a whole: they are inherently manipulable, and those who manipulate them rarely face consequences for doing so. That is not to say that Shakespeare supported monkeying with the law. We know that in his own life he was a frequent litigant,[9] so it is probably unlikely that he actually preferred a system that produced unjust results. But I suggest nevertheless that he was willing to point out the flaws he saw in the law whether or not he preferred it that way—and that his plays show that merely being right is not enough in the courtroom. Shylock has a quite clear contract; Katharine has a prior council decision saying that her initial marriage was valid (*Merchant* 4.1.227–9, *Henry VIII* 2.4.49–51). Their good legal arguments and their sympathetic stage presentation get them nothing. The only thing that would work would be to get the court itself on their side.

Court-packing

What implications might this have for Biden's presidency? I argue that Shakespeare's plays point to the inadequacy of mere argument in front of an unfriendly court. Merely trusting that the arguments you make are good law and make solid moral sense is not enough; it simply leads you to overestimate the chance you have to win without materially affecting how likely such a victory actually is. In other words, to win you have to change the game, not play with a stacked deck.

In terms of the modern Supreme Court, there is one major policy option that fits this bill: court-packing. Court-packing is the term for increasing the number of Supreme Court justices to overwhelm the current justices' positions and realign the court with the sensibilities of the elected parties in power. Since Supreme Court justices serve terms that are functionally for life, this means a sizable increase of justices, as the old ones cannot be easily removed.[10]

The first modern president to openly consider this was Franklin Delano Roosevelt, in the face of opposition to the New Deal.[11] He did not end up packing the court, because the court changed direction in the face of the threat.[12] But the idea was out there, and has been actively floated again in recent years.[13] Biden, in fact, appointed a commission to study what could be done about the court, which explicitly considered the possibility.

However, they did not actually issue a recommendation about whether to do it.[14] That decision to abstain has been widely criticized, including by some on the commission itself.[15] But in the wake of the report, any momentum for court-packing appears to have stalled, at least for the present.

But if Biden was to take the lessons of Shylock and Katharine seriously, I suggest, he would go ahead with the court-packing regardless (assuming, of course, that such a plan could pass the House and Senate—an assumption that, as we have seen above, is perhaps too generous). Those who oppose this move often speak as if the court was not a political body, and claim that judicial ethics and institutional norms are enough to make it impartial.[16] But Shakespeare's plays and recent court history both cast doubt on those assumptions.

Catering to self-interest

Recent Supreme Court history suggests that traditional institutional checks on the justices are not functioning in the way that they are supposed to. *Stare decisis*, the rule that precedents should, in general, be followed so that future litigants can assume that past decisions are settled law (a rule inherited from the England of Shakespeare's time), has been falling by the wayside;[17] court norms about deciding cases only after fully-briefed oral arguments, rather than on the so-called shadow docket of unargued or minimally argued opinions, have eroded rapidly;[18] and perhaps most concerningly the expectation of recusal in cases where the justice or their family have an interest has also been significantly weakened.[19]

The most recent major example of this is the case of Justice Clarence Thomas. Ginni Thomas, his wife, was found to be in direct communication with the White House Chief of Staff around the January 6 insurrection.[20] Justice Thomas, however, did not recuse himself from decisions about the release of White House records around similar communications—and was, in fact, the only dissenting vote arguing that they should not be released. Ethicists have pointed out that this appears to be a conflict of interest of the kind of conflict that a judge lower in the judicial hierarchy might be punished for.[21] But Thomas is not alone. Questions have been raised about the recusal practices of Justice Brett Kavanaugh as well,[22] and Chief Justice John Roberts recently signed on to an opinion that drew extensively on arguments he himself made as a member of the Reagan White House about voter rights to functionally eliminate a provision of the Voting Rights Act that he had unsuccessfully opposed at the time, thus using his new position to win an old argument.[23]

We might compare these situations to what we have already seen in Shakespeare above. The arguments made about Thomas's failure to recuse might remind us of Wolsey's claims to Henry VIII that he had nothing to do with initiating the divorce proceeding and so should not have to recuse or of Henry himself choosing the people who would judge his own divorce case, though I do not think such a direct parallel is actually useful (2.4.140–152). But I think that these issues of propriety and perception direct us also to another of Shakespeare's judicially-interested plays: *Measure for Measure*, and the corrupt judge Angelo.

Angelo is perceived, at first, as an upright judge. In 1.1, the Duke even commits the entire city into his charge because of that perception (1.1.15–23). He is somewhat overzealous in his pursuit of sin and vice, but the general assumption is that he is if anything too tough on crime: he follows the law too religiously, even where contemporary norms would suggest that he should let things slide (1.3.35–43).

But the play reveals that this is all false; Angelo is not what he seems. He blackmails Isabella into (what he thinks is) sex before marriage (2.4.88–98, 142–70). But it is not just a matter of a single slip into sexual assault and rape. It turns out that Angelo was always like this: he has abandoned a woman he promised to marry, and ultimately his main punishment from the Duke is to have to marry her (5.1.214–222, 374–5). Angelo did not merely have a moment of (horrific) weakness. This is how he operates, with seeming virtue covering vice.

I do not here intend to state that Angelo is a direct parallel for any current Supreme Court Justice, nor is this a sly attempt to wink at such a comparison coyly, without drawing it outright. Instead, I wish to point out that allowing Angelo to continue to serve while aware of all this behavior (a choice the Duke makes) is extremely problematic and in fact causes all the problems in the play. It is Angelo who instigates all of the difficulties that create the play's plot—Claudio's sentence, Isabella's conundrum—and the play is considered a problem play precisely because of his actions and how he is treated.

This should suggest, I argue, that the Shakespearean lesson here is not about any individual parallel, but about the dangers of allowing a corrupted judiciary to continue to judge. Angelo's threat to Viennese liberty increases the longer he is in power. From the initial decision to tear down brothels, which seems to actually have been part of the Duke's reason for giving him power in the first place, to threatening Claudio's life for a minor offense, to offering to spare it if Isabella sleeps with him, to reneging on the deal once he thinks she has, Angelo only gets worse.[24] And so the implication is, I believe, that this sort of self-dealing among judges only intensifies over time—and therefore must be cut off before it grows fully rotten.

It is highly unlikely that there is a two-thirds majority to impeach any current justice. Nor does Biden have the power that the Duke exercises at the end of *Measure for Measure* to unilaterally change, discharge, or otherwise alter judicial offices (5.1.458–9). A president is not a king, as we have seen; a president is also not Duke of Vienna. But while the remedy for current concerns about the court may not be as straightforward, that does not mean that doing nothing is sufficient. Whether that something is attempted impeachment, court-packing, the curtailment of Article III cases, or some other solution is not necessarily clear, as the commission's report shows.[25] But the lesson of Shakespeare's various self-interested judges and legal manipulations is much clearer: a damaged system will not heal itself. Even the Duke's return at the end of *Measure for Measure* only restores the already-corrupt system that was in place before the play, as many critics, particularly New Historicists, have noted.[26] Once the system is broken, it cannot be so simply made whole.

I suggest, then, that Shakespeare's plays show us that following our preferred legal norms in the face of corruption will not protect justice from a weakened or rotten judicial system. Whether considering the Republican takeover of the judiciary or the behavior of the justices currently in office, good wishes, good legal arguments, and a return to normalcy are not enough. Shakespeare shows that manipulating the legal system works. And just as importantly, the only effective counter he shows to such manipulation is to manipulate it right back. Isabella only defeats Angelo by playing a bed-trick on him and having the Duke, his superior, on her side (3.1.177–270). This is not a legal maneuver; rather, it is a counter-manipulation of the situation. If there is a lesson there for Biden, it is not to try to sleep with any of the justices. Rather, it is to consider his own manipulation of judicial norms and practices in response to the Republicans'—a response that most likely would begin by embracing court-packing and its related approaches.

Notes

1 Ian Milhiser, "What Trump has done to the courts, explained," *Vox*, September 29, 2020 (https://www.vox.com/policy-and-politics/2019/12/9/20962980/trump-supreme-court-federal-judges).
2 Tyler Olson, "Trump-appointed judges obstruct Biden 'pen and phone' policies just months into term," *Fox News*, June 26, 2021 (https://www.foxnews.com/politics/trump-appointed-judges-block-biden-policies).
3 Milhiser, "What Trump."
4 Charles Grassley, *Grassley Statement On The President's Nomination Of Merrick Garland To The U.S. Supreme Court* (https://www.grassley.senate.gov/news/news-releases/grassley-statement-presidents-nomination-merrick-garland-us-supreme-court).
5 Clare Foran and Ted Barrett, "Senate confirms Trump's Supreme Court nominee a week ahead of Election Day," *CNN*, October 26, 2020 (https://www.cnn.com/2020/10/26/politics/senate-confirmation-vote-supreme-court-amy-coney-barrett/index.html).
6 Gordon McMullan, introduction to *King Henry VIII (All Is True)*, William Shakespeare, ed. Gordon McMullan (London: Arden Shakespeare, 2000), 120–9.
7 Daniel J. Kornstein, *Kill All the Lawyers?: Shakespeare's Legal Appeal* (Princeton: Princeton University Press, 1994), 64–5; Richard H. Weisberg, "Lawyers and Judges Address Shylock's Case," in *Wrestling with Shylock: Jewish Responses to* The Merchant of Venice, ed. Edna Nahshon and Michael Shapiro (Cambridge: Cambridge University Press, 2017), 105–16.
8 Richard Strier, "Shakespeare and Legal Systems: The Better the Worse (But Not Vice Versa)," in *Shakespeare and the Law: A Conversation Among Disciplines and Professions*, ed. Bradin Cormack, Martha C. Nussbaum, and Richard Strier (Chicago: University of Chicago Press, 2013), 174.
9 Strier, "Legal Systems," 192.
10 US Constitution, Article III, Section 1.
11 Presidential Commission on the Supreme Court of the United States, *Final Report*, December 8, 2021, 54, 69.
12 Presidential Commission, *Final Report,* 55.
13 Presidential Commission, *Final Report*, 12–7.

14 Presidential Commission, *Final Report*, 82–3.
15 Madison Alder and Kimberly Strawbridge Robinson, "Biden's Supreme Court Commission Loses Two Conservatives," *Bloomberg Law,* October 15, 2021 (https://news.bloomberglaw.com/us-law-week/bidens-supreme-court-commission-looses-two-conservatives).
16 Mary Ramsey, "Justice Amy Coney Barrett argues US Supreme Court isn't 'a bunch of partisan hacks'," *Louisville Courier-Journal,* September 12, 2021 (https://www.courier-journal.com/story/news/politics/mitch-mcconnell/2021/09/12/justice-amy-coney-barrett-supreme-court-decisions-arent-political/8310849002/).
17 Henry Gass, "What Supreme Court's jettisoning of precedent may mean for future," *Christian Science Monitor,* May 20, 2021 (https://www.csmonitor.com/USA/Justice/2021/0520/What-Supreme-Court-s-jettisoning-of-precedent-may-mean-for-future).
18 Mark Walsh, "The Supreme Court's 'shadow docket' is drawing increasing scrutiny," *ABA Journal,* August 20, 2020 (https://www.abajournal.com/web/article/scotus-shadow-docket-draws-increasing-scrutiny).
19 Nina Totenberg, "Legal ethics experts agree: Justice Thomas must recuse in insurrection cases," *NPR,* March 30, 2022 (https://www.npr.org/2022/03/30/1089595933/legal-ethics-experts-agree-justice-thomas-must-recuse-in-insurrection-cases).
20 Totenberg, "Legal ethics."
21 Totenberg, "Legal ethics."
22 Jonathan Hurley, "Justice Kavanaugh unlikely to heed calls for recusal," *Reuters,* October 11, 2018 (https://www.reuters.com/article/us-usa-court-kavanaugh-recusal/justice-kavanaugh-unlikely-to-heed-calls-for-recusal-idUSKCN1ML18S).
23 Andy Kroll, "The Revenge of John Roberts," *Rolling Stone,* July 9, 2021 (https://www.rollingstone.com/politics/politics-features/supreme-court-john-roberts-voting-rights-brnovich-dark-money-1194487/).
24 Daniel Kornstein also notes this increasing "abuse of power" over time. Kornstein, *Kill*, 54–6.
25 Presidential Commission, *Final Report*, 7–10.
26 Rosalind Miles, *The Problem of* Measure for Measure (New York: Barnes and Noble, 1976), 284–5; A. R. Braunmuller and Robert N. Watson, introduction to *Measure for Measure*, William Shakespeare, ed. A. R. Braunmuller and Robert N. Watson (London: Arden Shakespeare, 2020), 54.

References

Alder, Madison and Kimberly Strawbridge Robinson. "Biden's Supreme Court Commission Loses Two Conservatives." *Bloomberg Law*, October 15, 2021 (https://news.bloomberglaw.com/us-law-week/bidens-supreme-court-commission-looses-two-conservatives).
Foran, Clare and Ted Barrett. "Senate Confirms Trump's Supreme Court Nominee a Week Ahead of Election Day." *CNN*, October 26, 2020 (https://www.cnn.com/2020/10/26/politics/senate-confirmation-vote-supreme-court-amy-coney-barrett/index.html).

Gass, Henry. "What Supreme Court's Jettisoning of Precedent May Mean for Future." *Christian Science Monitor*, May 20, 2021 (https://www.csmonitor.com/USA/Justice/2021/0520/What-Supreme-Court-s-jettisoning-of-precedent-may-mean-for-future).

Grassley, Charles. *Grassley Statement On The President's Nomination Of Merrick Garland To The U.S. Supreme Court* (https://www.grassley.senate.gov/news/news-releases/grassley-statement-presidents-nomination-merrick-garland-us-supreme-court).

Hurley, Jonathan. "Justice Kavanaugh Unlikely to Heed Calls for Recusal." *Reuters*, October 11, 2018 (https://www.reuters.com/article/us-usa-court-kavanaugh-recusal/justice-kavanaugh-unlikely-to-heed-calls-for-recusal-idUSKCN1ML18S).

Kornstein, Daniel J. *Kill All the Lawyers?: Shakespeare's Legal Appeal*. Princeton: Princeton University Press, 1994.

Kroll, Andy. "The Revenge of John Roberts." *Rolling Stone*, July 9, 2021 (https://www.rollingstone.com/politics/politics-features/supreme-court-john-roberts-voting-rights-brnovich-dark-money-1194487/).

McMullan, Gordon. Introduction to *King Henry VIII (All Is True)*, William Shakespeare, edited by Gordon McMullan, pp. 1–199. London: Arden Shakespeare, 2000.

Miles, Rosalind. *The Problem of* Measure for Measure. New York: Barnes and Noble, 1976.

Milhiser, Ian. "What Trump Has Done to the Courts, Explained." *Vox*, September 29, 2020 (https://www.vox.com/policy-and-politics/2019/12/9/20962980/trump-supreme-court-federal-judges).

Olson, Tyler. "Trump-appointed Judges Obstruct Biden 'Pen and Phone' Policies Just Months Into Term." *Fox News*, June 26, 2021 (https://www.foxnews.com/politics/trump-appointed-judges-block-biden-policies).

Presidential Commission on the Supreme Court of the United States, *Final Report*, December 8, 2021.

Ramsey, Mary. "Justice Amy Coney Barrett Argues US Supreme Court Isn't 'a Bunch of Partisan Hacks'." *Louisville Courier-Journal*, September 12, 2021 (https://www.courier-journal.com/story/news/politics/mitch-mcconnell/2021/09/12/justice-amy-coney-barrett-supreme-court-decisions-arent-political/8310849002/).

Shakespeare, William. *The Complete Oxford Shakespeare*, edited by Stanley Wells and Gary Taylor. Oxford: Oxford University Press, 1987.

Strier, Richard. "Shakespeare and Legal Systems: The Better the Worse (But Not Vice Versa)." In *Shakespeare and the Law: A Conversation Among Disciplines and Professions*, edited by Bradin Cormack, Martha C. Nussbaum, and Richard Strier, pp. 174–200. Chicago: University of Chicago Press, 2013.

Totenberg, Nina. "Legal Ethics Experts Agree: Justice Thomas Must Recuse in Insurrection Cases." *NPR*, March 30, 2022 (https://www.npr.org/2022/03/30/1089595933/legal-ethics-experts-agree-justice-thomas-must-recuse-in-insurrection-cases).

Walsh, Mark. "The Supreme Court's 'Shadow Docket' is Drawing Increasing Scrutiny." *ABA Journal*, August 20, 2020 (https://www.abajournal.com/web/article/scotus-shadow-docket-draws-increasing-scrutiny).

Weisberg, Richard H. "Lawyers and Judges Address Shylock's Case." In *Wrestling with Shylock: Jewish Responses to* The Merchant of Venice, edited Nahshon and Michael Shapiro, pp. 105–116. Cambridge: Cambridge University Press, 2017.

6 Lost France and Lost Afghanistan

Modern warfare bears little resemblance to the wars that Shakespeare saw in his own time or the ones he wrote about in his plays. Drones, airstrikes, and even accurate long-range guns have all remade the battlefield since then, not to mention radio, telephones, and the internet. But while the actual progress of a war is no longer Shakespearean, how we think about war as a society has not moved on nearly as far. Wars are still framed in terms of victory and loss, and the control of territory is frequently used to assess them, rather than any more complex measure.

In this regard, Shakespeare's plays about war—especially the seemingly endless English war with France—are still highly relevant to us today. How Shakespeare's medieval Englishmen thought about France is remarkably similar to how the American media today talks about Afghanistan. And this remains true even as a glance at a map shows how different the geopolitical situations that led to these wars truly were.

One of the most fraught decisions of Biden's early presidency—at least in the media telling of it—was the decision of whether and how to honor the agreement President Trump had made with the Taliban regarding the US withdrawal of troops from Afghanistan after twenty years. Initially, President Biden delayed the decision, moving a May 30 deadline for withdrawal to August 31. However, when faced with the return of the decision in August, he declined to delay any further and ordered the evacuation of all US troops by the deadline. As part of this process, US troops began to move out of the country in advance of the final deadline, ultimately leaving the Afghan army in charge of most of the bases where US troops had formerly been stationed, with the US in control of the Kabul airport, from whence evacuations were to take place.

Depending on your perspective on the situation on the ground in Afghanistan, this either prompted or revealed a massive deficit on the

DOI: 10.4324/9781003331391-7

part of the Afghan army, which not only proved incapable of holding the territory they were left in charge of but did not fight the Taliban at all in most instances, leading to a rapid collapse that brought the Taliban first to the gates of Kabul and then into the capital by the last week in August—before the US had fully completed its withdrawal from the country. Desperate supporters of the US presence and the Afghan government swarmed the airport, and the US was forced into a massive airlift operation to evacuate thousands upon thousands of people out of Kabul and the rest of the country.

A common response to this situation was to insist that Biden should have kept troops in the country. This was presented either as an insistence that he ought to have left the troops that were present after President Trump's agreement but before the actual withdrawal in August, or as a suggestion of "surging" more troops into Afghanistan—or to put it more bluntly, re-invading.

Biden refused both options and held firm on the withdrawal. On August 31, then, the last US troops left Afghanistan, though the evacuation effort continued for a few weeks afterwards, with the cooperation of the Taliban. The US lacked a military presence in Afghanistan for the first time since it and its NATO allies invaded Afghanistan in late 2001 in retaliation for Taliban support of Al-Qaeda, which had masterminded the attacks on 9/11.

The rhetoric around this move in the media quickly coalesced around a narrative that Biden had "lost" Afghanistan, with frequent comparisons to the fall of Saigon after the Vietnam War. This rhetoric would be oddly familiar to any student of Shakespeare because it sounds very much like the way that the nobles of England talk about France in Shakespeare's English history plays—with the exception of comparisons to the 1960s. Like Afghanistan, the answer to losing France was somehow always to throw more soldiers after the ones who had already died there—and also like the US in Afghanistan, it became increasingly difficult to say what, exactly, the English had actually had in France to lose besides mere physical presence.

In what follows, I will sketch out a brief summary of how Shakespeare's many plays about the English-French conflict treat the question of "lost France." I believe it is important for us to understand this context before trying to relate it back to our own time. If we do not know how these wars are different from our own, we cannot really understand why it matters when they are similar. But once that context is established, I will return to the American context to show how thinking about "lost France" can help us process our own "lost Afghanistan."

France forever lost

As we have seen, *Henry V* ends by undercutting Harry's triumph, re-minding us that he left the throne to his son, "Henry the Sixth, in infant bands crowned king/Of France and England .../Whose state so many had the managing/That they lost France and made his England bleed" (E.9–10, 11–12). The distinction between "lost France" and "*his* England" is not a casual but a causal one: France, unlike England, is not Henry's. "Lost France" may seem on the surface to suggest that France once *was* Henry's—but I suggest that a larger look at the English history plays shows that in fact France is always lost, and as such it was never England's, to begin with. The English possession of France is a ghost, always insubstantial: only the English war with and over France is fully realized.

In the three *Henry VI* plays, France is always already lost to England, even as the English strive to possess it. The first we hear of France in *1 Henry VI*, which opens with Henry V's funeral, is the news of its loss (1.1.58–61). The English peers respond to this by echoing forms of "loss" and "lost" (already used twice in the message) (1.1.63, 65, 68). There is, of course, a gesture here to the idea that France *should be* England's: you cannot lose something you never had. But even in context that is wishful thinking: a *second* messenger arrives almost immediately to tell them that France is actually even less English than they thought (1.1.90–2). At this point a *third* messenger arrives to remove all doubt. Now we have news not merely of France turning to Charles, but of war between England and France (1.1.105–6, 139). And we must remember that all of this *already happened* before the scene itself began, even if the lords are hearing of it now. Thus even as the play begins, the English have already lost France. The effect is that it was never truly theirs. *1 Henry VI* starts with the idea that France is not England's—and it only gets worse from there, ending with the "utter loss" of France by the end of the play (5.6.112).

The play consistently reminds us of the state of war between France and England, and while it might seem like the subject of that war is the claim that the English king is in fact also the king of France, this claim is frequently undercut both by the barbarism the English demonstrate towards their supposed co-subjects and by the rhetoric of who is English and who French and what that means. The English fight for Henry VI's "right," but they identify that right as "the right/Of English Henry," simultaneously making and unmaking the claim of Henry's Frenchness (2.1.35–6). In 3.1, Henry VI plans to be re-crowned king of France but does not achieve it until 4.1—and in the interim, the

French win over the Duke of Burgundy to join them in 3.7 precisely because he (unlike Henry) *is* French. Even the coronation scene itself descends back into a reminder of the fact that they "lost the realm of France!" (4.1.147). If Henry cannot keep up the pretense that he possesses France for a single scene, it should be no surprise that the English are more like an invading army than actual rulers of France (and indeed, he calls France "the conquest of my father" [4.1.148]). He is, as Talbot calls him in the next scene, "Harry, King of England" (4.2.4) more than he can ever even imagine himself to be Harry, King of France.

This emphasis on how insular England is and how France and it cannot truly be united continues into *2 Henry VI*. France is always already lost: just like the first play, this one opens with a scene revealing that France has been handed away offstage, with explicit references to losing it (1.1.100, 144, 214–6). This is echoed yet again in the third act, when Somerset announces that "all is lost" (3.1.85) while York specifies that "his highness hath lost France" (3.1.106). If the end of *1 Henry VI* had left any hope that France might be regained, *2 Henry VI* is committed to eliminating that hope and reminding the audience that France is for the French.

The practical reality of the situation, by this point, is that France is truly not Henry VI's realm in anything but name. If we needed more proof than the constant reiteration of its loss, the fact that Suffolk, upon being banished from Henry's territory, plans to take ship for France in 3.2 would confirm it. France can hardly be Henry's if this is a viable option. Or at least theoretically viable: Suffolk dies while trying to flee to France, but it is lawless pirates and not English authority over France that kills him.

These themes of distance and loss persist in the rest of the history plays. *Richard II* has the most famous reference to the sea barrier that divides true England and true France (John of Gaunt's speech about England as a perfect island would mean relatively little if half of the country were situated across the sea [2.1.31–68]) but the rest of them all touch on it as well. Warwick and the king again argue about who lost France at the start of *3 Henry VI* (1.1.110–4). By the third act, we are reminded once again that "Henry the Sixth hath lost/All that which Henry the Fifth had gotten" (3.3.89–90). Where Henry VI had at least theoretically married his French Queen Margaret for her father's "allegiance," Edward IV instead offers marriage for "alliance" implying that England no longer even pretends to have authority over France (*1 Henry VI* 5.7.43, *3 Henry VI* 3.3.177). By the end of the *Henry VI* plays, France is not only lost, but distanced, and while the later-written, earlier-set tetralogy has not *lost* France per se, as it never had it, the emphasis on distance persists throughout.

But while all thoughts of legitimately owning France may be put off until *Henry V*, two twinned themes remain that reinforce the idea of "lost France" in terms of marking France as an enemy and not a potential possession. These are the focus on the one hand on (badly) avoiding internal civil war, and on the other on fighting formal wars with France. The two are treated as interconnected not merely because Henry V uses the one to do the other, but because they consistently serve throughout the history plays as a contrasting couple: civil war is illegitimate, but the war in France is held up not as a civil war but as a proper war of conquest. This theme is present in the three *Henry VI* plays, from the infighting between Gloucester and Beaufort through the delays spurred by Somerset and York's disagreements that leave Talbot high and dry to the actual War of the Roses itself, each of which appears as the criticized counterbalance to battles against the French which are presented as more honorable. It recurs in *Richard III, Richard II*, and *Henry IV* plays not through actual contemporary fighting in France but through the memory of their fathers' days when they fought in France. In *King John*, it arrives through John's battle against Philip of France for Angiers, and the frequent revilement of the lords who revolt away from John to join Philip's son, Lewis, afterwards.

It is this contrast between the almost visceral need to attack, conquer, and defeat France on the one hand and the consistent emphasis on the horrors of civil war within England itself that most fully demarcates France as *always* lost, and never a true possession of England's. An English France is presented as the hoped-for possibility, the way out of the morass of the Hundred Years War: yet every time that the plays allow the audience to hope for this, they find themselves undercut and disappointed. This makes France seem like a mirage, often glimpsed but never grasped.

Ironically, this applies to the two plays where England triumphs over France just as much as it does to the plays where France is either too far away to think of or too lost to repossess. In *King John*, John's power is at its height when he routs the papally-inspired armies of Philip of France around Angiers. But he cannot conquer France: instead, upon his return to England he errs doubly by insisting on a second coronation (no more effective than Henry VI's) and doing violence to his nephew Arthur, whose claim to the throne he is resisting. These drive his people and his nobles away. At the same time, his mother dies and as a result, he loses all he had in France (4.2.128).

At the end of *King John*, the nobles come back; England triumphs; and John dies in the moment of his victory, handing the kingdom to his son Henry III. Yet this triumph and succession do not bring forward any claims in France, despite the earlier claims advanced in the first two acts. Rather, the closing message that the bastard Faulconbridge is left with is insular, a claim that England will never fall to outside conquest (5.7.112–118). England for the English, in other words, and not France.

We have already seen how *Henry V* ends with a reminder of the loss of France, thus devaluing the triumphal spirit of Henry's conquest. But even before that, *Henry V* is careful to make sure that its audience understands that France is not *really* England's by right, but an enemy to be conquered and subdued. From the first, there are "two mighty monarchies" in this play (P. 20). Even outside of the Prologue, the two priests Canterbury and Ely make clear in the first scene that the issue of Henry's right in France is being raised only to avoid increased taxation at home (1.1.71–85). Of course, when we do hear about that right, there is no discussion of the actual substance of Henry's inherited claim to France: while an Elizabethan audience *might* have known the rationale for Henry's claim, its absence from Canterbury's speech is notable. So too is his immediate pivot from right of blood to right of conquest (1.2.103–110). Henry decides to go to war before he claims the throne by right. There is no doubt the French would reject such a claim, as they do in 2.4, but Henry's rush to war, just like the play's failure to present his legal argument, reinforces the notion that France is an enemy to be conquered, and not actually a legitimate possession.

The war itself is as brutal as Henry promises it will be, and as the repression of the French in the *Henry VI* plays is. Bardolph is hanged for stealing a French pax, but this does not make Henry kind to his claimed subjects at Harfleur, which he promises to rape and pillage. He is waging war, not repossessing his own. Even Henry's victory does not actually make him king of France, only heir (5.2.335–6). While Queen Isabel of France hopes that this will mean "English may as French, French Englishmen/Receive each other" (5.2.363–4), we, the audience, and the Chorus all know that will not happen. Rather, we should remember her husband's description of them one speech earlier as "the contending kingdoms/Of France and England, whose very shores look pale/With envy of each other's happiness" (5.2.344–6)—or remember with the Chorus that Henry VI "lost France" because of the dissension of the English.

This lost France was, of course, more fully lost by Shakespeare's time. Even Calais, which remained in English hands until 1558, had fallen by the time any of these plays were performed, and while Elizabeth I may have styled herself Queen of England, France, and Ireland, there was no doubt that France was an enemy, not a real possession. Thus Shakespeare takes advantage of his audience's foreknowledge not only from his plays but from their own history to mark the pursuit of France in these plays as a Sisyphean task, one that would fall apart as the English fought each other instead of the French.

The Hundred Years War and the "forever war"

One major and important difference between the American and English contexts is that while the kings of England laid claim to the crown of France, America never claimed to have the right to actually own Afghanistan (unlike, say, Puerto Rico after the Spanish-American War). But as we have seen above, this difference is less material than it might initially appear when the full context of Shakespeare's plays is considered. While the English asserted a right to France, the English history plays make clear that they never truly possessed it, or even really thought of themselves as possessing it. France, for all it was *claimed* and even briefly legally *possessed*, was never truly considered a natural annex of the English throne. Perhaps Calais, which only returned to French control under Mary I, was an exception—but of course, American pundits and politicians were quick to claim that *parts* of Afghanistan should have been controlled indefinitely, most notably Bagram airbase.[1] Thus while the legal basis for the presence of troops in Shakespearean France and modern Afghanistan were wildly different, the conditions on the ground and the reactions to them among the political and military elite were more similar than they might at first appear. In both cases, the claim was that the "loss" of a foreign land symbolized the failure of the government, despite the fact that all involved ultimately acknowledged the impossibility of truly holding it.

The United States and its NATO allies officially did not invade Afghanistan for territorial conquest. The Authorization for the Use of Military Force that gave legal cover to the invasion was a direct response to the 9/11 attacks and the belief that Osama Bin Laden, who masterminded them, was being sheltered by the Taliban government in Afghanistan. After capturing Bin Laden proved elusive, the rationale for US presence shifted, but it never formally encompassed annexing or formally occupying the country—even though the twenty-year US presence in Afghanistan was approximately ten times as long as Henry V's possession of France had been.

However, that lack of formal claim to the territory of Afghanistan did not stop pundits and politicians from identifying withdrawal from Afghanistan as "losing" the country, in similar rhetoric to that used in Shakespeare about England's temporary French possessions. Of course, there was (and remains) some distinction of losing *the war* with losing *the country*, but with the rapid disintegration of the US-backed regime in Afghanistan in the midst of the US withdrawal that distinction became more and more blurred. Thus there were headlines asking "Who lost Afghanistan,"[2] echoed by the same question from Republican senators.[3] The same question reverberated through both sides of the political spectrum, from those accusing earlier presidents and military leaders to those blaming Biden, both for the decision to withdraw and for the withdrawal itself.

But if we take seriously the idea that Shakespeare's history plays can speak to our own time, we see that this is not, actually, a useful question. First of all, like Shakespeare's France, Afghanistan could not actually be lost, or perhaps was always lost, as it was never truly possessed to begin with. But we can draw a larger conclusion from the Shakespearean example as well: that arguing about losing Afghanistan, like arguing about losing France, is always a distraction from actually doing anything about the real issues of the day.

The obsession with lost France leads the English lords of the history plays to forget the importance of good governance at home (the "made his England bleed" of *Henry V*'s Chorus). It is used by a cudgel for different lords who wish to see themselves in charge of England, or their rivals removed, most notably in *1 Henry VI* when Cardinal Beaufort accuses Humphrey of Gloucester with it (among other charges, of course). Yet of course no one, except possibly Talbot, has any actual plan for *keeping* France; it is all about the optics of who is losing France, not the reality on the ground in France itself.

The same may be said about America's Afghanistan situation. Afghanistan was the centerpiece of what has been called the "forever war(s)" of America's 21st-century foreign policy.[4] The US had been in the country for almost the entirety of the century. But when they withdrew, the critique that Biden "lost Afghanistan" never came with a realistic road map to any other result.[5] Criticism of the withdrawal focused more on domestic political purposes than actual claims about how Afghanistan could have ended any differently (other than in a year with a different number).[6] Note, for instance, that Biden's withdrawal followed a roadmap agreed to by a Republican president, but the rhetoric from Republicans on the deal shifted significantly once it was a Democratic president implementing it.[7] At the same time, domestic coverage more generally focused on the impact of Biden's choices on American politics, and whether the choice to withdraw was wise within that context, rather than on the situation in Afghanistan.[8]

This is not to say that there could be no legitimate criticism of Biden's Afghanistan policy, any more than it is to suggest that the English commanders in France in Shakespeare's history plays behave perfectly. Rather, it is to suggest that comparing the one with the other can help us see the degree to which this particular criticism is weak. Afghanistan is not France; the Hundred Years War is not our Forever War. But the rhetoric of a perpetually lost possibility of an endless military presence is a common thread that might help us disentangle those legitimate criticisms, such as they are, from the kind of purely partisan rhetorical violence that brands the failure to perpetually control a foreign nation as "losing" that place—even when it was never there to be won.

This is, of course, a political strategy with a long history not just in Shakespeare but in America as well: the 1989 book *Lost Victory* painted the Vietnam War with the same brush, and the Cold War "Domino Theory" posited that other nations that the United States never had an actual interest in could be and would be lost to the specter of Communism if allowed to go their own way.[9] And in a sad twist that was not true when I began this writing, the same rhetoric has already ramped itself up about the Russian invasion of Ukraine.[10] But by looking at Shakespeare's "lost France," we can see just how ridiculous this kind of claim is. If the English were perpetually losing France because they never possessed it, how much more should America reject the idea that Afghanistan—or Ukraine—was ever ours, to begin with? These kind of arguments are primarily made with domestic political cudgeling in mind, but they have real-world consequences we can see in the chaos in France in Shakespeare's histories. Reinvading Afghanistan, or putting boots on the ground in Ukraine, would cost American blood and money just as the continual attacks on France in Shakespeare cost England. Pursuing "lost France" was part of what made Shakespeare's "England bleed." We should expect the same from any attempt to pursue a lost Afghanistan (or Ukraine) today.

Notes

1 Rob Crilly, "Erik Prince warns of more Kabul attacks and says U.S. should have kept Bagram air base open for evacuation not an airport in a city that can be shut by '10 guys with a couple of mortar tubes'," *Daily Mail*, August 26, 2021 (https://www.dailymail.co.uk/news/article-9930443/Erik-Prince-U-S-

kept-Bagram-air-base-open-evacuation-not-Kabul-airport.html); John Allen, "Biden must reverse his decision to quit Afghanistan," *DefenseOne*, 13 August 2021 (https://www.defenseone.com/ideas/2021/08/john-allen-biden-must-reverse-his-decision-quit-afghanistan/184512/); Meghann Myers, "Why Bagram wouldn't have made a difference, and more about the Afghanistan exit plan," *Military Times*, September 29, 2021 (https://www.militarytimes.com/flashpoints/afghanistan/2021/09/29/why-bagram-wouldnt-have-made-a-difference-and-more-about-the-afghanistan-exit-plan/).

2 Howard Kurtz, "Who lost Afghanistan? Why politicians and pundits may be asking the wrong question", Fox News, August 31, 2021 (https://www.foxnews.com/media/who-lost-afghanistan-why-politicians-and-pundits-may-be-asking-the-wrong-question); Daniel McCarthy, "Who lost Afghanistan?," Spectator World, August 29, 2021 (https://spectatorworld.com/topic/lost-afghanistan-withdrawal-joe-biden/).

3 Mitch McConnell, "Who lost Afghanistan? President Biden, Our Commander-in-Chief," August 18, 2021 (https://www.republicanleader.senate.gov/newsroom/research/who-lost-afghanistan-president-biden-our-commander-in-chief).

4 See for example Adam Kinzinger, "Ending the Forever Wars was never up to us," *Foreign Policy,* August 27, 2021. (https://foreignpolicy.com/2021/08/27/ending-the-forever-wars-was-never-up-to-us/); Paul Wolfowitz, "The 'Forever War' hasn't ended," *Wall Street Journal*, August 27, 2021 (https://www.wsj.com/articles/endless-war-afghanistan-withdrawal-biden-taliban-isis-mass-casualty-terror-attack-taiwan-11630076447).

5 David Rothkopf, "There's chaos and risk in Afghanistan exit, but Biden critics are getting it mostly wrong," *USA Today*, August 29, 2021, (https://www.usatoday.com/story/opinion/2021/08/29/afghanistan-war-exit-joe-biden-critics-wrong/5639051001); David Rothkopf, "Biden Deserves Credit, Not Blame, for Afghanistan," *The Atlantic*, August 30, 2021 (https://www.theatlantic.com/ideas/archive/2021/08/biden-deserves-credit-not-blame-for-afghanistan/619925/); Charles A. Kupchan, "Biden Was Right," *Council on Foreign Relations*, August 16, 2021 (https://www.cfr.org/article/biden-was-right).

6 See for example Cristina Marcos and Scott Wong, "Republicans hit Biden over Afghanistan, with eye on midterms," *The Hill*, August 29, 2021 (https://thehill.com/homenews/house/569812-republicans-hit-biden-over-afghanistan-with-eye-on-midterms). One potential exception is Jennifer Brick Murtazashvili's argument that the collapse of Afghanistan was not inevitable—but she too points primarily to decisions made in 2001–4, not 2021. Jennifer Brick Murtazashvili, "The Collapse of Afghanistan," *Journal of Democracy* 33, no. 1 (2022), pp. 40–54.

7 JM Rieger, "The GOP's shifts in tone and substance on the Afghanistan withdrawal," *Washington Post*, September 3, 2021 (https://www.washingtonpost.com/politics/2021/09/02/republicans-afghanistan-withdrawal/).

8 Ashley Parker, Tyler Pager, and Sean Sullivan, "The long slide: Inside Biden's declining popularity as he struggles with multiple crises," *Washington Post*, January 19, 2022 (https://www.washingtonpost.com/politics/biden-decline-first-year/2022/01/18/19ecd8c0-7557-11ec-8ec6-9d61f7afbe17_story.html).

9 William Colby and James McCargar, *Lost Victory: A Firsthand Account of America's Sixteen-Year Involvement in Vietnam* (Chicago: Contemporary Books, 1989).
10 Rana Foroohar and Edward Luce, "Biden, Trump and the 'who lost Ukraine' debate," *Financial Times*, FT Swamp Notes, February 25, 2022 (https://www.ft.com/content/8e473bf9-1222-468d-82a6-080e78bf44c6).

References

Allen, John. "Biden Must Reverse His Decision to Quit Afghanistan." *DefenseOne*, August 13, 2021 (https://www.defenseone.com/ideas/2021/08/john-allen-biden-must-reverse-his-decision-quit-afghanistan/184512/).

Brick Murtazashvili, Jennifer. "The Collapse of Afghanistan." *Journal of Democracy* 33, no. 1 (2022): 40–54.

Colby, William and James McCargar. *Lost Victory: A Firsthand Account of America's Sixteen-Year Involvement in Vietnam.* Chicago: Contemporary Books, 1989.

Crilly, Rob. "Erik Prince Warns of More Kabul Attacks and Says U.S. Should Have Kept Bagram Air Base Open for Evacuation Not an Airport In a City that Can Be Shut by '10 Guys With a Couple of Mortar Tubes'." *Daily Mail*, August 26, 2021 (https://www.dailymail.co.uk/news/article-9930443/Erik-Prince-U-S-kept-Bagram-air-base-open-evacuation-not-Kabul-airport.html).

Foroohar, Rana and Edward Luce, "Biden, Trump and the 'Who Lost Ukraine' Debate." *Financial Times*, FT Swamp Notes, February 25, 2022 (https://www.ft.com/content/8e473bf9-1222-468d-82a6-080e78bf44c6).

Kinzinger, Adam. "Ending the Forever Wars Was Never Up to Us." *Foreign Policy*, August 27, 2021 (https://foreignpolicy.com/2021/08/27/ending-the-forever-wars-was-never-up-to-us/).

Kupchan, Charles A. "Biden Was Right." *Council on Foreign Relations*, August 16, 2021 (https://www.cfr.org/article/biden-was-right).

Kurtz, Howard. "Who Lost Afghanistan? Why Politicians and Pundits May be Asking the Wrong Question.", *Fox News*, August 31, 2021, (https://www.foxnews.com/media/who-lost-afghanistan-why-politicians-and-pundits-may-be-asking-the-wrong-question).

Marcos, Cristina and Scott Wong, "Republicans Hit Biden Over Afghanistan, with Eye on Midterms," *The Hill*, August 29, 2021 (https://thehill.com/homenews/house/569812-republicans-hit-biden-over-afghanistan-with-eye-on-midterms).

McCarthy, Daniel. "Who Lost Afghanistan?," *Spectator World*, August 29, 2021, https://spectatorworld.com/topic/lost-afghanistan-withdrawal-joe-biden/

McConnell, Mitch. "Who Lost Afghanistan? President Biden, Our Commander-in-Chief." August 18, 2021 (https://www.republicanleader.senate.gov/newsroom/research/who-lost-afghanistan-president-biden-our-commander-in-chief).

Myers, Meghann. "Why Bagram Wouldn't Have Made a Difference, and More About the Afghanistan Exit Plan." *Military Times*, September 29, 2021 (https://www.militarytimes.com/flashpoints/afghanistan/2021/09/29/why-bagram-wouldnt-have-made-a-difference-and-more-about-the-afghanistan-exit-plan/).

Parker, Ashley, Tyler Pager, and Sean Sullivan "The long slide: Inside Biden's Declining Popularity As He Struggles With Multiple Crises." *Washington Post*, January 19, 2022 (https://www.washingtonpost.com/politics/biden-decline-first-year/2022/01/18/19ecd8c0-7557-11ec-8ec6-9d61f7afbe17_story.html).

Rieger, J.M. "The GOP's Shifts in Tone and Substance on the Afghanistan Withdrawal." *Washington Post*, September 3, 2021 (https://www.washingtonpost.com/politics/2021/09/02/republicans-afghanistan-withdrawal/).

Rothkopf, David. "Biden Deserves Credit, Not Blame, for Afghanistan." *The Atlantic*, August 30, 2021 (https://www.theatlantic.com/ideas/archive/2021/08/biden-deserves-credit-not-blame-for-afghanistan/619925/).

Rothkopf, David. "There's Chaos and Risk in Afghanistan Exit, But Biden Critics are Getting It Mostly Wrong." *USA Today*, August 29, 2021, (https://www.usatoday.com/story/opinion/2021/08/29/afghanistan-war-exit-joe-biden-critics-wrong/5639051001).

Shakespeare, William. *The Complete Oxford Shakespeare*, edited by Stanley Wells and Gary Taylor. Oxford: Oxford University Press, 1987.

Wolfowitz, Paul. "The 'Forever War' Hasn't Ended." *Wall Street Journal*, August 27, 2021 (https://www.wsj.com/articles/endless-war-afghanistan-withdrawal-biden-taliban-isis-mass-casualty-terror-attack-taiwan-11630076447).

Conclusion: Shakespeare and Presentism

Obviously, this book is not the be-all and the end-all of how Shakespeare applies to the present. I have focused here on DC politics, with their parallels to the high-level politics Shakespeare often depicted in his plays. But that has meant passing by innumerable pressing topics that critics, audiences, and readers have connected to Shakespeare. Perhaps most obviously, I have not accounted for Shakespeare's relevance to either contemporary or premodern ideas of race, gender, sexuality, or class.[1] Nor have I looked at other significant elements of contemporary politics that Shakespeare relates to, such as immigration, abortion, police violence, or the current pandemic, even those these issues too "color and vitalize our experience with Shakespeare," as Ruben Espinosa and David Ruiter have put it.[2] This book, then, is deliberately a sketch of an approach to presentism through a certain kind of politics and not a comprehensive examination of all presentist readings. By limiting its scope, I hope to have made that approach clear: how we might look at Shakespeare's texts for contemporary relevance not by simple parallelism or the kind of citational opportunism that seizes on a single quote or a single figure but by looking at the larger implications of how Shakespeare explored his own, carefully drawn worlds.

In other words, I want to suggest that Shakespeare's connection to our present day comes not from a simple universalism that erases the imagined reality of the political and social worlds the plays create, but through an attentive embrace of those worlds. Shakespeare had a careful eye for political dynamics, and as such the plays each represent their own situations in a meaningful way. To bridge the gap between us and them—or between us and Shakespeare's own time—we must acknowledge how the plays depict individuals reacting to individual circumstances, and extrapolate from there. We cannot search among Shakespeare's characters, hoping to rip off a mask in the style of Scooby-Doo and find our contemporaries hiding underneath. Julius

DOI: 10.4324/9781003331391-8

Caesar is not Donald Trump. Instead, we must think carefully about what makes us want to look for that parallel and how it might translate across the difference in time, place, and politics: consider how *Julius Caesar*'s factionalism might inform our views of our own partisanship, and what the consequences of that factionalism in the play mean for our future. It is not because "Shakespeare depersonalized Caesar" that we can see Shakespeare's Caesar in our politics.[3] Rather, it is because Shakespeare drew Caesar's world as a real world, and so we can see how it might be similar to ours—and how both the similarities and the differences matter.

We read Shakespeare's plays in the present. They were written in the past. They depict yet other pasts and other societies. To interpret Shakespeare fully in the present requires us to acknowledge all three of these elements simultaneously. It asks us to think about what made them, them, and what makes us, us. And while we necessarily privilege the present in that thinking—note that this book does not ask much of *Much Ado About Nothing*, for example, beyond the treatment of Don John, even though that is definitely not the dominant theme of the play—we should not forget the other elements along the way. Shakespeare is not our contemporary. But his insight into political actions, motivations, and consequences can still help us think about the people who are.

Notes

1 It would not be possible to cover all of these fields in one note, or one book, but I will supply some recent places to start a deeper exploration. For race, the vital work of the RaceB4Race group at the Arizona Center for Medieval and Renaissance Studies is a place to start, especially the issue "Race Before Race: Premodern Critical Race Studies" in *Literature Compass* 18, no. 10 (2021). For gender and sexuality, Evelyn Gajowski's introductory essay "The Presence of the Past" in *Presentism, Gender, and Sexuality in Shakespeare*, ed. Evelyn Gajowski (New York: Palgrave Macmillan, 2009), pp. 1–24 and Sawyer K. Kemp, "'In That Dimension Grossly Clad': Transgender Rhetoric, Representation, and Shakespeare," *Shakespeare Studies* 47 (2019): 120–126 both give brief overviews of relatively recent work and directions for new exploration. For class, *Shakespeare and the 99%: Literary Studies, the Profession, and the Production of Inequity*, ed. Sharon O'Dair and Timothy Francisco (Cham, Switzerland: Palgrave Macmillan, 2019) provides a good introduction.

2 Ruben Espinosa and David Ruiter, introduction to *Shakespeare and Immigration*, ed. Rubin Espinosa and David Ruiter (London: Routledge, 2014), 10.

3 Wilson, *Trump*, 135.

References

Espinosa, Ruben and David Ruiter. Introduction to *Shakespeare and Immigration*, edited by Rubin Espinosa and David Ruiter, pp. 1–12. London: Routledge, 2014.

Gajowski, Evelyn. "The Presence of the Past." In *Presentism, Gender, and Sexuality in Shakespeare*, edited by Evelyn Gajowski, pp. 1–24. New York: Palgrave Macmillan, 2009.

Kemp, Sawyer K. "'In That Dimension Grossly Clad': Transgender Rhetoric, Representation, and Shakespeare." *Shakespeare Studies* 47 (2019): 120–126.

"Race Before Race: Premodern Critical Race Studies." *Literature Compass* 18, no. 10 (2021).

Shakespeare and the 99%: Literary Studies, the Profession, and the Production of Inequity. Edited by Sharon O'Dair and Timothy Francisco. Cham, Switzerland: Palgrave Macmillan, 2019.

Wilson, Jeffrey. *Shakespeare and Trump*. Philadelphia: Temple University Press, 2020.

Index

Page numbers followed by "n" indicate notes.